Magical
WOODLAND
KNITS

Knitting patterns for
12 wonderfully lifelike animals

CLAIRE GARLAND

DAVID & CHARLES

www.davidandcharles.com

Contents

Welcome
TO THE WOOD

To me the woods is a world within, and apart from, this world.

It's the subject of the darker side of fairy tales, where weary travellers rest awhile around campfires, always wary of what could be lurking amongst the tall trees, or nestling, unseen, within their gnarly roots and under the hollow ground.

It's a land where one could tiptoe silently on freshly fallen snow only to tumble headfirst down into a badger's lavishly furnished holt, or stumble blindly into a lamp post and then take tea with a charming fellow with cloven hooves.

It's where elves and pixies and fairies dwell in toadstool houses and fern covered shelters.

This is the magic of the woods where the living creatures nestle amongst the toadstools and fern covered shelters, in hollows and under the snowy ground, without any knowledge of the world outside this foresty habitat.

These are the animals that I've tried to capture within the pages of this book and that you too can create with a few balls of yarn and a pair of knitting needles. You can also read some rather fascinating folklore facts about the animals including the deer and the rabbit, the wolf, the fox and the badger and not forgetting the smaller creatures: the birds and the mouse and, of course the wise old owl.

Welcome to my Magical Woodland World!

Claire Garland

How to Use This Book

Yarn

To create the colours and textures for the creatures in this book I combine different coloured and textured yarns which are held together to knit.

Within the patterns, the yarn combinations are written as follows:

- Yarn **ABC** means one strand each of yarns **A**, **B** & **C**.

- Yarn **EEF** means 2 strands of yarn **E** and one of yarn **F**.

- Yarn **J** means just one strand of yarn **J**.

To work with two strands of the same yarn, you can take the second strand from the other end of the ball.

Casting on and casting off

Cable cast-on and standard cast-off are used throughout these patterns unless otherwise stated.

Using lockable stitch markers

I use lockable stitch markers to mark points that will be joined, or to show where to pick up stitches. Always put the marker into a stitch rather than on the needle.

Sewing up

To sew the seams, choose a yarn that matches one side of the seam.

For small seams (e.g. around an eye socket), use a single strand of kid mohair.

For longer seams, use a single strand of 4ply yarn (or DK yarn for patterns knit with DK).

Many seams need to be eased to get the two sides to fit together. I do this to create the curves of the animal. It helps if you pin these seams before sewing.

Eyes

For most of the projects in this book I have used 'toy safety eyes' which are plastic (or resin) eyes. These come with either with metal or plastic washer backs which you push on to fix them in place.

For the mouse's eyes, I used the type that you have to glue in place. To fit the eye I created a hole where I wanted the eye to go (using a tapestry needle) then applied glue to the stem of the eye and pushed the eye into the hole wriggling it around a bit to make sure the glue adhered well inside the hole.

Stuffing

I use a heavier weight stuffing, which gives the knitted creature more weight and therefore allows it to sit more naturally. It's easier to pose and sculpt too.

How much stuffing? That depends on which part I am stuffing.

For a face I tend to use a bit less to create a gentle bagginess that occurs around the jowls and around the eye sockets.

For the body, however, I use more, especially around the haunches of the wolf and fox for example. This enhances the curved shape and helps the backbone to look like a real spine.

A top tip is to leave a tiny gap in the very last seam you sew then you can add or remove stuffing as you live with your new friend for a while.

Supporting structures

Some of the knitted creatures need a little extra support.

I used rolled-up strips of paper as a support, in forelegs for example, or a tiny rolled up strip inside the pheasant's beak.

I rarely use wire because it always pokes through. The only times it's used in this book is for the duck beak and the pheasant's tail. In both places I bent it into a loop to close up the sharp cut edges.

Bird legs

The larger birds use purchased bird legs. These are simple to use, just insert and then glue into place. They can be bent into shape to create life-like legs and toes (white legs are easier to bend than black ones), and the colour can be changed using florist's tape or yarn.

The large white legs that I use come as a joined pair which is great for stability, but you can clip them apart with pliers if you wish.

Sculpting

This is the part that I spend the most time on and it's the most enjoyable and rewarding part of the whole process. I've finished the knitting, I've sewn the seams, stuffed the head and body, added the ears and fitted in the eyes… and then I sculpt.

By sculpting I mean moulding the knitted creature to make it look as life-like as possible. This means pushing my thumbs into eyes sockets, pulling and bending feet to enhance paw shapes, squeezing and twisting waists to shape the belly and breast. It might seem quite brutal, but it's worth it for the result.

For finer details, like tiny beaks or mouse legs I dampen the knitting slightly and use my fingers to tease and shape the knitting.

Sometimes I will also add a tiny concealed stitch here and there, to join the squirrel's tiny paws together, or defining the widow's peak on the barn owl.

Important

These patterns are not intended as toys.

However, they could be made for small children if you leave out any wire or other hard or sharp parts, and use felt or embroidery for the eyes. You may also want to consider using washable yarns and stuffing.

Tools and Materials

Yarn

These yarns are used in this book, the colours required are specified within the patterns.

- Drops Alpaca: 100% Alpaca, 167m (183yds) per 50g

- Drops Baby Alpaca Silk: 70% Alpaca, 30% Silk 167m (183yds) per 50g

- Drops Brushed Alpaca Silk: 77% Alpaca, 23% Silk, 140m (153yds) per 25g

- Drops Flora: 65% Wool, 35% Alpaca, 210m (230yds) per 50g

- Drops Karisma: 100% Wool, 100m (109yds) per 50g

- Drops Kid Silk: 75% Mohair, 25% Silk, 210m (230yds) per 25g

- Drops Lima: 65% Wool, 35% Alpaca, 100m (109yds) per 50g

- Drops Nord: 45% Alpaca, 30% Polyamide, 25% Wool, 170m (186yds) per 50g

- Drops Safran: 100% Cotton, 160m (175yds) per 50g

- James C Brett Faux Fur: 90% Nylon, 10% Polyester, 90m (98yds) per 100g

- King Cole Luxury Fur: 90% Nylon, 10% Polyester, 92m (100yds) per 100g

- Rico Essentials Super Kid Mohair Loves Silk: 70% Mohair, 30% Silk, 200m (218yds) per 25g

If you want to substitute different yarns, it is important to stick to similar yarn types (e.g. a 4ply yarn for a 4ply yarn, a fur yarn for a fur yarn), and check your tension using the yarn combinations from the pattern.

Needles

These patterns are written for straight needles but could be knit using circular needles if desired.

Tools

- Stitch holders or safety pins to hold stitches.

- Locking stitch markers.

- A tapestry needle for sewing up.

- Pins to hold longer seams together while you sew them.

- Scissors.

Materials

Stuffing

Heavy uncarded polyester fibre filling.

Or, you can use yarn and fabric scraps, but be sure to cut them into very small pieces.

Toy safety eyes

There are a huge variety of eyes available, so take time to find the right colour and iris shape for your woodland creature. In my experience, the more expensive ones are better quality.

Wire bird legs

For the Pheasant and Barn Owl I used the large white glue-in legs (2cm (¾in) wide by 5cm (2in) high).

Florist's tape

Used to cover wire bird legs.

Wire

Used in Pheasant's tail and Duck's bill.

Glue

I use a glue stick. It's less messy than PVA and easier to apply.

UK to US Terms

UK	US
cast off	bind off
stocking stitch	stockinette
tension	gauge

Needle Conversion Chart

UK	Metric	US
-	2.5mm	1.5
12	2.75mm	2
11	3mm	-
10	3.25mm	3
-	3.5mm	4
9	3.75mm	5
8	4mm	6
7	4.5mm	7
6	5mm	8

Abbreviations

k: knit

k2tog: knit two stitches together as one

k3tog: knit three stitches together as one

kfb: knit into the front and back of one stitch

LH: left hand

m1: make one: with LH needle pick up a loop between stitches from the front, then knit into the back of it

p: purl

p2tog: purl two stitches together as one

p3tog: purl three stitches together as one

pfb: purl into the front and back of one stitch

PM: place marker

RH: right hand

RS: right side of work

skpo: slip, knit, pass over: slip one stitch as if to knit, knit the next stitch, pass the slip stitch over the knit stitch and off the needle

sl: slip stitch purlwise

st(s): stitch(es)

WS: wrong side of work

W+T: wrap and turn (see General Techniques)

stocking stitch: knit on RS rows, purl on WS rows

garter stitch: knit every row

[ ]: indicates a repeat sequence

Projects

Wild Rabbit

{Oryctolagus cuniculus}

The rabbit is the clever, darting trickster of the woods, almost always outwitting his enemy or adversary. Cannily getting the better of his foe… probably due to his knack of being so silent, not a single trodden footstep will you hear.

FINISHED SIZE

Approx. 30cm (12in) tall

YARN:

You will need no more than one ball each of:

A: Drops Alpaca in shade 0618 light beige mix

B: Drops Kid Silk in shade 15 dark brown

C: Drops Alpaca in shade 2923 goldenrod

D: Drops Flora in shade 07 beige

E: Drops Flora in shade 02 white

F: Drops Kid Silk in shade 01 off white

G: Drops Flora in shade 20 peach pink

Unless otherwise stated, multiple strands of yarn are used together throughout this pattern. The exact combinations of yarn to be used are indicated by multiple letters (see How to Use This Book).

NEEDLES

3.75mm knitting needles, plus one extra needle

TENSION

15 rows and 11 stitches over 5cm (2in) with 3.75mm knitting needles

OTHER TOOLS AND MATERIALS

· 2 stitch holders

· 20 locking stitch markers

· 18mm brown toy safety eyes

· Toy filling or yarn/fabric scraps

BEGINNING AT THE NOSE

With yarn **ABC**, cast on 10 sts.

Row 1 (RS): Kfb, k4, turn, so purl-side is facing you, to work on left muzzle - 6sts

Row 2 (WS): P6

Row 3: Kfb, k4, kfb, turn, cast on 2sts for nose, turn, k4 sts across right muzzle, kfb - 16sts

Row 4: P6, turn to work on right muzzle

Row 5: Kfb, k4, kfb - 18sts

Row 6: Purl across all sts (i.e right muzzle, nose and left muzzle)

Row 7: Kfb, k6, [kfb] 4 times, k6, kfb - 24sts

Row 8: Purl

Row 9: Kfb, k to last st, kfb - 26sts

Row 10: Purl

Row 11: K10, kfb, k4, kfb, k to end - 28sts

Row 12: Purl

Row 13: K14, m1, k to end - 29sts

Row 14: Purl

PM at each end of last row for **Chin Marker**.

Cut **C** and join **D** to work with yarn **ABD**.

Separate top nose from cheeks:

Row 15 (RS): K20, turn, so WS is facing you

Row 16 (WS): P11, turn, so RS is facing you

TOP OF NOSE AND FOREHEAD

Working on these middle 11 sts:

Row 17: K3, kfb, k3, kfb, k3 - 13sts

Row 18: P13

Row 19: K4, kfb, k3, kfb, k4 - 15sts

Row 20: P15

Row 21: K5, kfb, k3, kfb, k5 - 17sts

Rows 22-25: Work 4 rows stocking stitch

Row 26: P2tog, p13, p2tog - 15 forehead sts

Cut yarns and leave these 15 sts on a stitch holder.

CHEEKS

Rabbit's Right Cheek

With RS facing you, return to the 9 sts (on your left), rejoin yarn **ABD**.

Row 1 (RS): Knit

Row 2: P2tog, p5, p2tog - 7sts

Rows 3-6: Work 4 rows stocking stitch

Row 7: Cast on 3 sts, knit to end - 10sts

Row 8: P10

Cut all 3 yarns and leave these 10 sts on a stitch holder.

Rabbit's Left Cheek

With WS facing you, return to the remaining set of 9 sts, rejoin yarn **ABD**.

Row 1 (WS): P2tog, p5, p2tog - 7sts

Rows 2-5: Work 4 rows stocking stitch

Row 6: K7, turn, cast on 3 sts - 10sts

Row 7: P10, turn

TOP AND SIDES OF HEAD

Row 1 (RS): K10 from rabbit's left cheek; slip the 15 forehead sts from the stitch holder onto LH needle with RS facing you, k15; slip 10 right cheek sts from the stitch holder onto LH needle with RS facing you, k10 - 35sts

Row 2: P2tog, purl to last 2 sts, p2tog - 33sts

Rows 3-6: Work 4 rows stocking stitch

Row 7: Cast off 9 sts, k6, slip the next 17 sts onto a stitch holder.

EARS

Rabbit's Left Ear

Work the 7 sts for the left ear:

Row 1 (WS): Cast on 7 sts, p14 - 14sts

Cut **B** and continue with yarn **AD**:

Row 2: Kfb, k to last st, kfb - 16sts

Row 3: Purl

PM at each end of last row for left **Ear Marker**

Rows 4-7: Repeat last 2 rows twice - 20sts

Row 8: K1, skpo, k to last 3 sts, k2tog, k1 - 18sts

Row 9: Purl

Rows 10-17: Repeat last 2 rows four times - 10sts

Rows 18-21: Work 4 rows stocking stitch

Row 22: K4, [kfb] twice, k4 - 12sts

Row 23: Purl

Row 24: Skpo, k2, k2tog, skpo, k2, k2tog - 8sts

Row 25: Purl

Row 26: Skpo, k4, k2tog - 6sts

Row 27: Purl

Row 28: K2tog all across - 3sts

Row 29: P3tog

Fasten off.

Rabbit's Right Ear

With RS facing you slip just the first 8 sts from the stitch holder onto a knitting needle.

With yarn **ABD**, work the right ear:

Row 1 (RS): Cast on 7 sts, k7, k2tog, k6 - 14sts

Row 2: Purl

PM at each end of last row for right **Ear Marker**

Cut **B** and continue with yarn **AD**:

Row 3: Kfb, k to last st, kfb - 16sts

Row 4: Purl

Rows 5-8: Repeat last 2 rows twice - 20sts

Row 9: K1, skpo, k to last 3 sts, k2tog, k1 - 18sts

Row 10: Purl

Rows 11-18: Repeat last 2 rows four times - 10sts

Rows 19-22: Work 4 rows stocking stitch

Row 23: K4, [kfb] twice, k to end - 12sts

Row 24: Purl

Row 25: Skpo, k2, k2tog, skpo, k2, k2tog - 8sts

Row 26: Purl

Row 27: Skpo, k4, k2tog - 6sts

Row 28: Purl

Row 29: K2tog all across - 3sts

Row 30: P3tog

Fasten off.

SIDE OF HEAD

With RS facing you slip the remaining 9 sts from the stitch holder onto a knitting needle.

Rejoin yarn **ABD**, and cast off all sts.

INNER EARS

Rabbit's Left Ear

Outside edge

With RS facing you, with yarn **FG** pick up and knit 12 sts (see General Techniques) from the left **Ear Marker** to the fastened off tip of the ear (*see fig. 1, A to B*).

Row 1 (WS): Purl

Row 2: K to last 2 sts, k2tog - 11sts

Rows 3-6: Repeat last 2 rows twice - 9sts

Row 7: Purl

Cast off.

Inside edge

With RS facing you, with yarn **FG** pick up and knit 12 sts from the tip of the ear to the left **Ear Marker** (*see fig. 1, C to D*).

Row 1 (WS): Purl

Row 2: K1, skpo, k to end - 11sts

Rows 3-6: Repeat last 2 rows twice - 9sts

Row 7: Purl

Cast off.

Rabbit's Right Ear

Inside edge

With RS facing you, with yarn **FG** pick up and knit 12 sts from the right **Ear Marker** to the fastened off tip of the ear (*see fig. 1, E to F*).

Row 1: Purl

Row 2: K to last 2 sts, k2tog - 11sts

Rows 3-6: Repeat last 2 rows twice - 9sts

Row 7: Purl

Cast off.

Outside edge

With RS facing you, with yarn **FG** pick up and knit 12 sts from the tip of the ear to the right **Ear Marker** (*see fig. 1, G to H*).

Row 1: Purl

Row 2: K1, skpo, k to end - 11sts

Rows 3-6: Repeat last 2 rows twice - 9sts

Row 7: Purl

Cast off.

Working on one ear inner at a time, with RS together, match the cast-off edges of the inside edge and outside edge and back stitch to join along the cast-off edge, and then the diagonal row ends up to the tip of the ear (*see fig. 2, dotted line from A to B*). Leave the straight edges at the base of the ear inner open for turning through.

Turn out to RS and trim the tails ends (it's best not to have any stuffing for inside the ears).

Fold each ear in half, tucking the inner ear inside the fold, so that the **Ear Markers** meet and mattress stitch to join the base from the **Ear Marker** to the fold (*see fig. 2, C*).

Remove the **Ear Markers**.

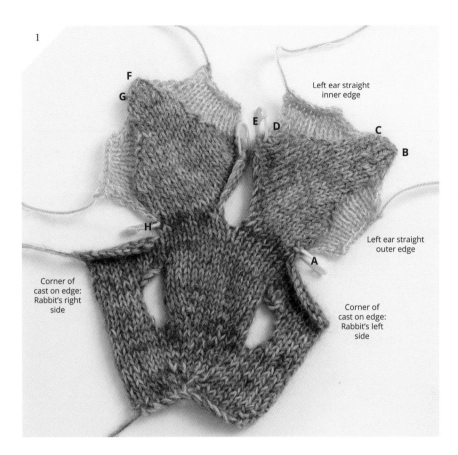

1

F

G

Left ear straight inner edge

E D

C

B

Left ear straight outer edge

A

H

Corner of cast on edge: Rabbit's right side

Corner of cast on edge: Rabbit's left side

2

B

A

C

3

B

A

4

A

B

Fold nose in half RS together across the cast-on edge and back stitch to join the cast-on edge (*see fig. 3, dotted line from A to B*). Turn out to RS (*see fig. 4, dotted line from A to B*).

BACK OF HEAD AND NECK

With the back of the ears and head facing you, ears towards you, and with yarn **AD**, pick up and knit 16 sts across the backs of both ears (*see fig. 5, dotted line from A to B*).

Row 1 (WS): Purl
Row 2: K4, skpo, k2, k2tog, k to end - 14sts
Rows 3-5: Work 3 rows stocking stitch
Row 6: K3, skpo, k2, k2tog, k to end - 12sts
Rows 7-9: Work 3 rows stocking stitch
Row 10: K2, skpo, k2, k2tog, k to end - 10sts
Row 11: Purl

Leave sts on their needle for now and don't cut the yarn.

NECK

Note: In this section you are working with two different yarn combinations in the same rows. The yarn not in use should be carried across the back on the work to the next place it is needed.

With RS toward you and beginning at rabbit's left **Chin Marker**, with yarn **EF**, pick up and knit 8 sts from the **Chin Marker** to corner of the cast-off edge (*see fig. 1*); with yarn **AD** knit across the 10 sts from the head back; with yarn **EF** pick up and knit 8 sts from the corner of the cast-off edge on rabbit's right (*see fig. 1*) to the right **Chin Marker** - 26sts

Row 1 (WS): P8 in **EF**; p10 in **AD**; p8 in **EF**
Row 2: K8 in **EF**; k2, skpo, k2, k2tog, k2 in **AD**; k8 in **EF** - 24sts
Row 3: P8 in **EF**; p8 in **AD**; p8 in **EF**
Cut **EF** and join on **B** to work with yarn **ABD**.
Row 4: K10, skpo, k2tog, k to end - 22sts
Row 5: Purl

Working on one side at a time, mattress stitch the seam that runs from beneath the base of the ears and down the neck (*see fig. 6, A to B*).

SHOULDERS

Continue with yarn **ABD**.
Row 6 (RS): Cast on 7sts, k16, kfb, k2, kfb, k9, turn, cast on 7sts - 38sts
Row 7: Purl
Row 8: K1, kfb, k15, kfb, k2, kfb, k to

last 2 sts, kfb, k1 - 42sts

Row 9: Purl

Row 10: K1, kfb, k17, kfb, k2, kfb, k to last 2 sts, kfb, k1 46sts

Rows 11-15: Work 5 rows stocking stitch
PM at each end last row for **Foreleg Marker**.

Row 16: K1, skpo, k17, skpo, k2, k2tog, k to last 3 sts, k2tog, k1 - 42sts

Row 17: P2tog, purl to last 2 sts, p2tog - 40sts

Row 18: K1, skpo, k to last 3 sts, k2tog, k1 - 38sts

Rows 19-20: Repeat last 2 rows once - 34sts

Rows 21-23: Work 3 rows stocking stitch starting with a purl row
PM at each end last row for **Under-Foreleg Marker**.

Row 24: K1, kfb k to last 2 sts, kfb, k1 - 36sts

Row 25: Purl

Rows 26-27: Repeat last 2 rows once - 38sts

Join **C** to work with yarn **ABCD**.

Row 28: K1, kfb, k to last 2 sts, kfb, k1 - 40sts

Row 29: Purl

Row 30: K1, kfb k to last 2 sts, kfb, k1 - 42sts

Row 31: Purl

Row 32: K1, kfb, k17, k2tog, k to last 2 sts, kfb, k1 - 43sts

Row 33: Purl

Row 34: K1, kfb, k17, k3tog, k to last 2 sts, kfb, k1

Row 35: Purl

Rows 36-37: Repeat last 2 rows once

Row 38: K20, k3tog, k to end - 41sts

Row 39: Purl
PM at each end last row for **Hind Leg Marker**.

HIND LEGS - UPPER PART

Rabbit's Left Leg

Cut **D** to work with yarn **ABC**.

Cast on 6 sts - 47sts, then work short rows (see General Techniques) to create the top of the left leg:

Short row 1: K7, W+T
Short row 2: P1, W+T
Short row 3: K2, W+T
Short row 4: P3, W+T
Short row 5: K4, W+T
Short rows 6-11: Continue as set, working longer rows each time until…
Short row 12: P11, W+T
Short row 13: K21, k3tog, knit to end - 45sts

Rabbit's Right Leg

Cast on 6 sts - 51sts, then work short rows to create the top of the right leg:

Short row 1: P7, W+T
Short row 2: K1, W+T
Short row 3: P2, W+T
Short row 4: K3, W+T
Short row 5: P4, W+T
Short rows 6-11: Continue as set, working longer rows each time until…
Short row 12: K11, W+T
Short row 13: Purl to end
Row 40: K24, k3tog, k to end - 49sts
Row 41: Purl
Row 42: K23, k3tog, k to end - 47sts
Row 43: Purl
Row 44: K22, k3tog, k to end - 45sts
Row 45: Purl
Separate lower back from hind legs:
Row 46 (RS): K21, k3tog, k12, turn
Row 47: P2tog, p21, p2tog, turn

LOWER BACK

Working on the 23 sts for Lower Back:
Row 48 (RS): K10, k3tog, k10, turn - 21 lower back sts
Row 49: P21, turn
Row 50: K9, k3tog, k9, turn - 19 lower back sts
Row 51: Purl the lower back sts, turn
Row 52: K8, k3tog, k8, turn - 17 lower back sts
Row 53: Purl the lower back sts, turn
Row 54: K7, k3tog, k7, turn - 15 lower back sts
Row 55: Purl the lower back sts, turn
Row 56: K6, k3tog, k6, turn - 13 lower back sts
Row 57: Purl the lower back sts, turn

TAIL

Cut all yarns and join on yarn **EEF**, to work just on the 13 sts of the lower back:
Row 1 (RS): K13
Row 2: Purl the tail sts
Row 3: K3, kfb, k5, kfb, k3 - 15 tail sts
Row 4: Purl the tail sts
Row 5: K4, kfb, k5, kfb, k4 - 17 tail sts
Row 6: Purl the tail sts
Row 7: K5, kfb, K5, kfb, k5 - 19 tail sts
Row 8: Purl
Row 9: K3, skpo, k9, k2tog, k3 - 17 tail sts
Row 10: P2tog, purl to last 2 tail sts, p2tog - 15 tail sts

5

6

Row 11: K3, skpo, k5, k2tog, k3 - 13 tail sts
Row 12: P2tog, purl to last 2 tail sts, p2tog - 11 tail sts
Row 13: K3, skpo, k1, k2tog, k3 - 9 tail sts
Row 14: P2tog, purl to last 2 tail sts, p2tog - 7 tail sts
Cast off 7 tail sts leaving a long tail end to sew the seam with.
With RS together, fold tail in half across the cast-off edge and match rows ends.

Back stitch across the cast-off edge and down row ends to join just the tail seam (seam will be at the underside of the tail).

Turn out to RS, and tuck yarn ends back in through the tail as stuffing.

HIND LEGS - LOWER PART

Rabbit's Right Hind Leg

With RS facing you, rejoin yarn **ABC** to the 9 sts held on left-hand needle.
Rows 1-8: Work 8 rows stocking stitch
Cast off.

Rabbit's Left Hind Leg

With WS facing you, rejoin yarn **ABC** to the 9 sts held on left-hand needle.
Rows 1-8: Work 8 rows stocking stitch starting with a purl row
Cast off purlwise.

Working on one side at a time, with RS together, ease the back stitch along row ends to join lower back to hind legs from split to beginning of white tail *(see fig. 7, A to B)*.

FRONT

With yarn **DEF** with RS facing you, starting at the corner of the cast-off edge from left leg *(see fig. 8, C)* pick up and knit 5 sts along the cast-off edge, pick up and knit 3 sts under and across the base of the tail, then pick up and knit 5 sts across cast-off edge of right leg to corner *(see fig. 8, D)*.
Row 1 (WS): P4, p2tog, p1, p2tog, purl to end - 11sts
Row 2: K4, k3tog, k to end - 9sts
Row 3: Purl
Row 4: K2, kfb, k3, kfb, k to end - 11sts
Row 5: Purl
Row 6: K2, kfb, k5, kfb, k to end - 13sts
Row 7: Purl
Row 8: K2, kfb, k7, kfb, k to end - 15sts
Row 9: Purl
Row 10: K2, kfb, k9, kfb, k to end - 17sts
Row 11: Purl
Row 12: K2, kfb, k11, kfb, k to end - 19sts
Row 13: Purl
Work short rows to shape belly:
Short row 1: K13, W+T
Short row 2: P7, W+T
Short row 3: K6, W+T
Short row 4: P5, W+T
Short row 5: K4, W+T
Short row 6: P3, W+T
Short row 7: Knit to end
Row 14 (WS): Purl
Row 15: Kfb, k1, kfb, k to last 3 sts, kfb, k1, kfb - 23sts
Rows 16-17: Repeat last 2 rows once - 27sts
Row 18: Purl
Row 19: K1, kfb, k to last 2 sts, kfb, k1 - 29sts
Row 20: Purl
Work short rows to create the inner thighs:
Short row 1: K26, W+T
Short row 2: P23, W+T
Short row 3: K22, W+T
Short row 4: P21, W+T
Short row 5: K20, W+T
Short row 6: P19, W+T
Short row 7: K18, W+T
Short row 8: P17, W+T
Short row 9: K16, W+T
Short row 10: P15, W+T
Short row 11: K14, W+T
Short row 12: P13, W+T
Short row 13: Knit to end
Row 21 (WS): P2tog, purl to last 2 sts, p2tog - 27sts
Row 22: K5, skpo, k13, k2tog, k5 - 25sts
PM at each end last row for **Inner Thigh Marker**.
Row 23: P2tog, purl to last 2 sts, p2tog - 23sts
Row 24: K3, skpo, k13, k2tog, k3 - 21sts
Row 25: P2tog, purl to last 2 sts, p2tog - 19sts
Row 26: K1, skpo, k to last 3 sts, k2tog, k1 - 17sts
Row 27: Purl
Row 28: Skpo, k to last 2 sts, k2tog - 15sts
Row 29: Purl
Cut **D** and join on **E**, to work with yarn **EEF**.

Rows 30-33: Work 4 rows stocking stitch PM at each end of last row for **Breast Marker**.

Row 34: Cast off 2 sts, k to end - 13sts

Row 35: Cast off 2 sts purlwise, purl to end - 11sts

Row 36: Skpo, k to last 2 sts, k2tog - 9sts.

Row 37: Purl

Rows 38-39: Repeat last 2 rows once - 7sts

Cast off all sts.

BREAST AND CHIN

With RS facing you and with yarn **EEF**, starting at the left **Breast Marker**, pick up and knit 14 sts across the left side row ends, the cast-off edge, and the right side row ends, to the right **Breast Marker**.

Remove **Breast Markers**.

Row 1 (WS): Purl

PM at each end of last row for **White Under-Foreleg Marker**.

Row 2: Kfb, k to last st, kfb - 16sts

Row 3: Purl

Row 4: K1, skpo, k to last 3 sts, k2tog, k1 - 14sts

Row 5: Purl

Rows 6-9: Repeat last 2 rows twice - 10sts.

PM at each end of last row for **White Foreleg Marker**.

Rows 10-11: Work 2 rows stocking stitch.

Row 12: K1, kfb, k to last 2 sts, kfb, k1 - 12sts.

Row 13: Purl

Rows 14-19: Repeat last 2 rows three times - 18sts

Row 20: Kfb, k to last st, kfb - 20sts

Row 21: Purl

Row 22: Cast off 2 sts, k to end - 18sts

Row 23: Cast off 2 sts purlwise, purl to end - 16sts

Row 24: Skpo, k to last 2 sts, k2tog - 14sts

Rows 25-27: Beginning with a purl row work 3 rows stocking stitch

PM at each end of last row for **White Chin Marker**.

Row 28: Skpo, k1, k2tog, k4, skpo, k1, k2tog - 10sts

Row 29: Purl

Row 30: K2, skpo, k2, k2tog, k2 - 8sts

Row 31: Purl

Row 32: K2, skpo, k2tog, k2 - 6sts

Row 33: [P2tog] 3 times - 3sts

Row 34: K3tog.

Fasten off.

EYES

Note: It's best to knit and sew in one eye at a time.

Rabbit's Left Eye

With yarn **EEF**, cast on 1 stitch.

Row 1 (RS): Kfb - 2sts

Row 2: Purl

Row 3: Kfb, k1 - 3sts

Row 4: Purl

Row 5: Kfb, k2 - 4sts

Row 6: Purl

Row 7: Kfb, k2, kfb - 6sts

Row 8: Purl

Row 9: Skpo, k2, k2tog - 4sts

Row 10: Purl

Row 11: Skpo, k2tog - 2sts

Row 12: P2tog

Fasten off.

Note: Fasten off point is the front of the left eye.

Attach the toy eye in the centre of the knitted eye (*see fig. 9*), then insert the knitted eye into the left eye socket and using one strand of yarn **A**, carefully whip stitch around the eye to join it into the eye socket

Rabbit's Right Eye

With yarn **EEF**, cast on 1 st

Row 1 (RS): Kfb - 2 sts

Row 2: Purl

Row 3: K1, kfb

Row 4: Purl

Row 5: K2, kfb - 4sts

Row 6: Purl

Row 7: Kfb, k2, kfb - 6sts

Row 8: Purl

Row 9: Skpo, k2, k2tog - 4sts

Row 10: Purl

Row 11: Skpo, k2tog - 2sts

Row 12: P2tog

Fasten off.

Note: Fasten off point is the back of the right eye.

Attach the toy eye to the knitted eye and insert into right eye socket as before.

9

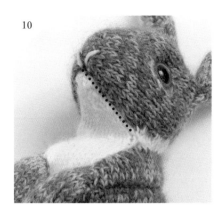

10

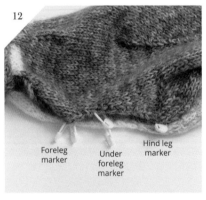

11

White foreleg

Foreleg marker

Under foreleg marker

12

Foreleg marker

Under foreleg marker

Hind leg marker

13

Right foreleg marker

SEWING CHEEKS TO CHIN

With RS facing you and working on one side of the face at a time, match the end of the nose seam to the fastened off end of the front, and the **Chin Marker** to the **White Chin Marker**, and mattress stitch from the end of the nose seam to the **Chin Markers** (*see fig. 10*).

Tuck in yarn ends and stuff the head, making sure that the stuffing aids with the shaping of the cheeks and nose.

Using yarn **A**, embroider straight lines for the nose and the mouth.

SEWING THE BACK TO THE FRONT

With RS facing you and working on one side of the body at a time:

Match the **Foreleg Marker** to the **White Foreleg Marker**, and mattress stitch from the **Chin Markers** (which can now be removed) to the **Foreleg Markers**.

Match the **Under-Foreleg Marker** to the **White Under-Foreleg Marker** and the **Hind Leg Marker** to the **Inner Thigh Marker**. Leave gaps for forelegs between the **Foreleg Marker** and the **Under-Foreleg Marker** then mattress stitch from the **Under-Foreleg Marker** to the tail (*see figs. 11 and 12*).

Remove markers as you come to them but leave one **Foreleg Marker** and one **Under-Foreleg Marker** on each side of the rabbit.

Note: You may find it helpful to pin these seams before sewing.

Before completing the second side, tuck in yarn ends and stuff the rabbit carefully - not too much, not too little - what you are looking for is gently shaping with an element of firmness but not fatness.

FORELEGS - MAKE 2 ALIKE

With yarn **ABD**, cast on 8 sts leaving a long tail end join leg to body

Row 1 (RS): [K2, kfb] twice, k2 - 10sts

Rows 2-13: Beginning with a purl row work 12 rows stocking stitch

Work short rows to create the foreleg paw:

Short row 1: P9, W+T
Short row 2: K8, W+T
Short row 3: P7, W+T
Short row 4: K6, W+T
Short row 5: P5, W+T
Short row 6: K4, W+T
Short row 7: P3, W+T
Short row 8: K2, W+T
Short row 9: Purl to end

Cast off leaving a long tail end to sew the seam with.

With WS together fold foreleg in half across the cast-off edge and mattress stitch along the cast-off edge. Match the row ends, and mattress stitch from the cast-off edge to the cast-on edge.

Tuck in yarn ends and stuff fairly firmly then slip the cast-on edge inside the body at the armholes, between the **Foreleg Markers**, and whip stitch around each leg to join it to the breast, removing **Foreleg Markers** as you sew (*see fig. 13*).

HIND LEG FEET - MAKE 2 ALIKE

With yarn **ABC** cast on 9 sts leaving a long tail end to join foot to leg.

Rows 1-6: Work 6 rows stocking stitch
Row 7: K3, kfb, k1, kfb, k to end - 11sts
Row 8: Purl
Row 9: K4, kfb, k1, kfb, k to end - 13sts
Row 10: Purl
Row 11: K5, kfb, k1, kfb, k to end - 15sts
Row 12: Purl
Row 13: K6, kfb, k1, kfb, k to end - 17sts
Row 14: Purl

Cut **C** and join on **E** to work with yarn **ABE**.

Row 15: K7, kfb, k1, kfb, k to end - 19sts
Row 16: Purl
Row 17: K8, kfb, k1, kfb, k to end - 21sts
Rows 18-26: Work 9 rows stocking stitch
Row 27: K5, skpo, k7, k2tog, k5 - 19sts
Row 28: P2tog, purl to last 2 sts, p2tog - 17sts
Row 29: K4, skpo, k5, k2tog, k4 - 15sts
Row 30: P2tog, purl to last 2 sts, p2tog - 13sts
Row 31: K3, skpo, k3, k2tog, k3 - 11sts
Row 32: P2tog, purl to last 2 sts, p2tog - 9sts
Row 33: K2, skpo, k1, k2tog, k2 - 7sts
Row 34: P2tog, purl to last 2 sts, p2tog - 5sts
Row 35: K1, k3tog, k1 - 3sts

Cut yarn leaving a long tail end with which to join seam, thread end through all sts.

With WS together fold hind leg in half across the cast-off edge and mattress stitch along the cast-off edge. Match the row ends, and mattress stitch from the cast-off edge to the cast-on edge.

Tuck in yarn ends and stuff fairly firmly, then whip stitch the cast-on edge to the body back - just behind the front seam.

Using yarn **A**, embroider stitches for the toes.

FINISHING TOUCHES

Finally, to make the face squish up a little, fold a length of yarn in half and pass the cut ends through a yarn sewing needle. Pass the threaded needle through one side of the head, halfway between the ears and chin, and out the other side of the head, about 2.5cm (1in) away. Then pass the needle back through the head to emerge back out where you started and through the loop of the folded yarn. Pull up to squish the face and secure the thread.

Grey Squirrel

{Sciurus carolinensis}

According to Norse Mythology a squirrel
can travel across an entire country without
once touching the ground, and for this reason
they gained employment carrying news
and ferrying insults between the eagle, the
denizen of the World Tree, and the dragon
inhabiting the roots of the Underworld.

FINISHED SIZE

Approx. 17cm (6¾in) tall

YARN

You will need no more than one ball each of:

A: Drops Alpaca in shade 0501 light grey mix

B: Drops Brushed Alpaca Silk in shade 02 light grey

C: Drops Brushed Alpaca Silk in shade 19 curry

D: Drops Alpaca in shade 0517 medium grey mix

E: Drops Kid Silk in shade 10 grey

F: Drops Flora in shade 02 white

G: Drops Kid Silk in shade 01 off white

H: James C Brett Faux Fur Chunky in shade H2 grey/white

I: Drops Flora in shade 20 peach pink

J: Drops Kid Silk in shade 15 dark brown

Unless otherwise stated, multiple strands of yarn are used together throughout this pattern. The exact combinations of yarn to be used are indicated by multiple letters (see How to Use This Book).

NEEDLES

3.75mm knitting needles

TENSION

15 rows and 11 stitches over 5cm (2in) with 3.75mm knitting needles

OTHER TOOLS AND MATERIALS

· 2 safety pins or stitch holders

· 14 locking stitch markers

· 9mm black oval toy safety eyes

· Toy filling or yarn/fabric scraps

BEGINNING AT THE MUZZLE

With yarn **AB** cast on 9 sts.

Work short rows (see General Techniques) to create the squirrel's left muzzle:

Short row 1: K3, W+T
Short row 2: P3
Short row 3: K2, W+T
Short row 4: P2
Short row 5: K1, W+T
Short row 6: P1
Row 1: Knit

Work short rows to create the squirrel's right muzzle:

Short row 1: P3, W+T
Short row 2: K3
Short row 3: P2, W+T
Short row 4: K2
Short row 5: P1, W+T
Short row 6: K1
Row 2: Purl

Cut **B** and join **C** to work with yarn **AC**.

Row 3: [Kfb, k1] four times, kfb -14sts
Row 4: Purl

FOREHEAD

Row 5: [K4, kfb] twice, turn
Row 6: P8, turn

Working on just these 8 sts for the forehead:

Row 7: Kfb, k6, kfb, turn - 10 forehead sts
Row 8: P10, turn

Join **B** to work with yarn **ABC**.

Row 9: Kfb, k8, kfb, turn - 12 forehead sts
Rows 10-12: Work 3 rows stocking stitch starting with a purl row

Cut yarn and leave the 12 forehead sts on a safety pin.

CHEEKS

Squirrel's Right Cheek

With RS facing you, with yarn **AB** return to the 4 sts on squirrel's right (on your left).

Row 1: Knit
Row 2: P3, pfb - 5 sts

PM at start of last row for right **Chin Marker**.

Rows 3-4: Work 2 rows stocking stitch

Cut yarn and leave all 5 right cheek sts on a safety pin.

Squirrel's Left Cheek

With WS facing you, with yarn **AB** return to the 4 sts on squirrel's left (on your right).

Row 1: Pfb, purl to end - 5sts

PM at end of last row for left **Chin Marker**.

Rows 2-3: Work 2 rows stocking stitch

Join Cheeks to Forehead

Row 4: K5 left cheek sts, slip the 12 forehead sts onto LH needle with RS facing you, k12, slip the 5 right cheek sts onto LH needle with RS facing you, k5 - 22sts
Row 5: Purl, pulling tension taut as you purl across the joins

Work short rows to shape the back of the head:

Short row 1: K15, W+T
Short row 2: P8, W+T
Short row 3: K7, W+T
Short row 4: P6, W+T
Short row 5: K5, W+T
Short row 6: P4, W+T
Short row 7: Knit to end
Row 6: Purl

Divide for Ear Spaces

Row 7: K3, cast off next 4 sts for squirrel's left **Ear Space**, skpo, k2, k2tog, k1, cast off next 4 sts for squirrel's right **Ear Space**, knit to end - 12sts
Row 8: P3, turn, cast on 3 sts, turn, p2tog, p2, p2tog, turn, cast on 3 sts, turn, p3 to end - 16sts
Row 9: Knit
Row 10: P1, p2tog, purl to last 3 sts, p2tog, p1 - 14sts
Cast off all sts for **Neck Back**.

NECK AND BACK

With RS facing you, return to the squirrel's left. With yarn **AB** pick up and knit 7 sts (see General Techniques) from the squirrel's left **Chin Marker** to the corner of the **Neck Back** cast-off edge (*see fig. 1, dotted line A to B*), backward loop cast on 5 sts for Neck Back, pick up 7 sts from corner of the **Neck Back** cast-off edge (*see fig. 2*), along to squirrel's right **Chin Marker** - 19sts

Row 1: Purl
Row 2: Kfb, knit to last st, kfb - 21sts
Row 3: P9, p3tog, purl to end - 19sts
Row 4: Kfb, knit to last st, kfb - 21sts
Row 5: Purl
Join **C** to work with yarn **ABC**.
Row 6: Kfb, k8, kfb, k1, kfb, knit to last st, kfb - 25sts
Row 7: Purl

Forelegs

Row 8: PM for **Neck Marker**, cast on 7 sts for squirrel's left foreleg, PM for **Foreleg Marker**, k18, kfb, k1, kfb, knit to end - 34sts
Row 9: PM for **Neck Marker**, cast on 7 sts for squirrel's right foreleg, PM for **Foreleg Marker**, purl to end - 41sts
Row 10: K19, kfb, k1, kfb, knit to end - 43sts
Row 11: Purl
Row 12: K20, kfb, k1, kfb, knit to end - 45sts
Row 13: Purl
Row 14: K21, kfb, k1, kfb, knit to end - 47sts
Row 15: Purl
Row 16: Cast off 7 sts for squirrel's left foreleg, knit next 14sts, kfb, k1, kfb, knit to end - 42sts
Row 17: Cast off 7 sts purlwise for squirrel's right foreleg, purl to end - 35sts
Cut **AB** and join **D** to work with yarn **CD**.
Row 18: K2tog, knit to last 2 sts, k2tog - 33sts
Row 19: Purl
Row 20: K2tog, knit to last 2 sts, k2tog - 31sts
Row 21: Cast off 6 sts for right **Side Seam**, purl to end - 25sts
Row 22: Cast off 6 sts for left **Side Seam**, knit to end - 19sts
Row 23: Cast on 5 sts for right **Side Seam**, purl to end - 24sts
Row 24: Cast on 5 sts for left **Side Seam**, knit to end - 29sts

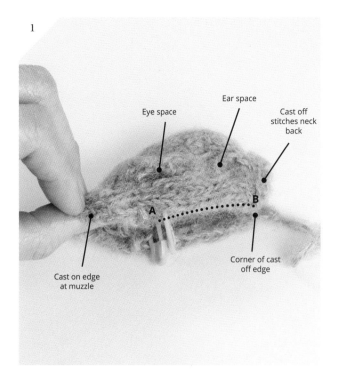

1

Eye space
Ear space
Cast off stitches neck back
A
B
Cast on edge at muzzle
Corner of cast off edge

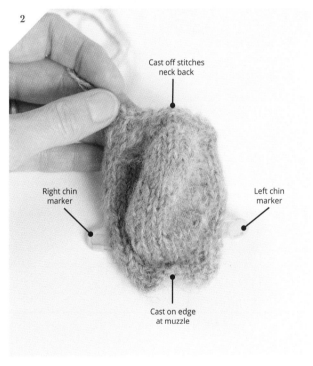

2

Cast off stitches neck back
Right chin marker
Left chin marker
Cast on edge at muzzle

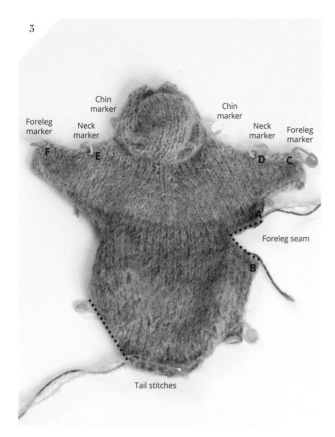

3

Chin marker

Chin marker

Foreleg marker

Neck marker

Neck marker

Foreleg marker

F   E   D   C

A

Foreleg seam

B

Tail stitches

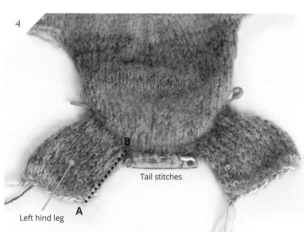

4

B

Tail stitches

Left hind leg

A

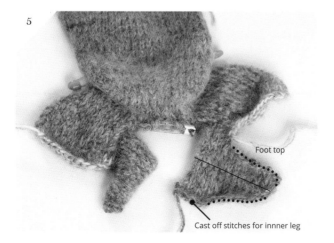

5

Foot top

Cast off stitches for inner leg

Rows 25-31: Work 7 rows stocking stitch starting with a purl row

Rump

Join **B** to work with yarn **BCD**.

Work short rows to shape the rump:

Short row 1: K28, W+T
Short row 2: P27, W+T
Short row 3: K26, W+T
Short row 4: P25, W+T
Short row 5: K24, W+T
Short row 6: P23, W+T
Short row 7: K9, skpo, k1, k2tog, k8, W+T
Short row 8: P19, W+T
Short row 9: K18, W+T
Short row 10: P17, W+T
Short row 11: K6, skpo, k1, k2tog, k5, W+T
Short row 12: P13, W+T
Short row 13: K12, W+T
Short row 14: P11, W+T
Short row 15: Knit to end
Row 32: Purl all 25 sts

PM at each end of last row for **Thigh Markers**.

Row 33: Cast off 6 sts for squirrel's left hind leg thigh, knit next 12 sts, cast off last 6 sts for right hind leg thigh - 13sts

With WS facing you, rejoin yarn **BCD**.

Row 34: P2tog, purl to last 2 sts, p2tog - 11sts.
Row 35: K2tog, knit to last 2 sts, k2tog - 9sts
Row 36: Purl
Rows 37-38: Repeat last two rows once - 7sts.

Cut yarn and leave all 7 tail sts on a safety pin.

Sewing Neck Back and Side Seams

Return to the back of the neck, with RS together match the **Neck Back** cast-off stitches with the cast-on stitches. Ease together and back stitch to join.

Note: You may find it easier if you pin the seam before sewing. Working on one side at a time, with RS together, match the **Side Seam** cast-off edge with the **Side Seam** cast-on edge, and back stitch to join *(see fig. 3, dotted line A to dotted line B)*.

HIND LEGS

Squirrel's Left Hind Leg

With RS facing you, with yarn **BDE** pick up and knit 10 sts from the squirrel's left **Thigh Marker** to the tail stitches held on the safety pin (*see fig. 3*).

Row 1: Purl
Row 2: Kfb, knit to end - 11sts
Rows 3-6: Repeat last 2 rows twice - 13sts
Row 7: Purl

Work short rows to shape the haunches:

Short row 1: Kfb, k11, W+T - 14sts
Short row 2: P13
Short row 3: Kfb, k11, W+T - 15sts
Short row 4: P13
Short row 5: K12, W+T
Short row 6: P12
Short row 7: K11, W+T
Short row 8: P11

Cut **D** and join **F** to work with yarn **BEF**.

Row 8: K2tog, knit to end - 14sts
Row 9: Purl
Row 10: K2tog, knit to end - 13sts

PM at end of last row for **Foot Marker**.

Cast off purlwise for the front of the left hind leg.

Squirrel's Right Hind Leg

With RS facing you, with yarn **BDE** pick up and knit 10 sts from the tail stitches held on the safety pin to the right **Thigh Marker**.

Row 1: Purl
Row 2: Knit to last st, kfb - 11sts
Rows 3-6: Repeat last 2 rows twice 13sts

Work short rows to shape the haunches:

Short row 1: Pfb, p11, W+T - 14sts
Short row 2: K13
Short row 3: Pfb, p11, W+T - 15sts
Short row 4: K13
Short row 5: P12, W+T
Short row 6: K12
Short row 7: P11, W+T
Short row 8: K11
Row 7: Purl

Cut **D** and join **F** to work with yarn **BEF**.

Row 8: Knit to last 2 sts, k2tog - 14sts
Row 9: Purl
Row 10: Knit to last 2 sts, k2tog - 13sts

PM at start of last row for **Foot Marker**.

Cast off purlwise for the front of the right hind leg.

HIND LEG FEET

Squirrel's Left Hind Foot

With RS facing you, with yarn **BDE** pick up and knit 6 sts from squirrel's left **Foot Marker** to the tail stitches held on the safety pin (*see fig. 4, dotted line from A to B*).

Row 1: Purl
Row 2: Cast on 6 sts for Left Foot, knit to end - 12sts
Row 3: Purl
Row 4: Kfb, knit to end - 13sts
Row 5: Purl
Rows 6-7: Repeat last 2 rows once - 14sts
Row 8: Knit
Row 9: Purl to last 2 sts, p2tog - 13sts
Rows 10-13: Repeat last 2 rows twice - 11sts
Row 14: Cast off 5 sts for left **Foot Top**, knit to end - 6sts
Rows 15-16: Work 2 rows stocking stitch starting with a purl row

Cast off all 6 sts for left **Inner Leg**.

Squirrel's Right Hind Foot

With RS facing you, with yarn **BDE** pick up and knit 6 sts from the tail stitches held on the safety pin to squirrel's right **Foot Marker**.

Row 1: Purl
Row 2: Knit
Row 3: Cast on 6 sts for Left Foot, purl to end - 12sts
Row 4: Knit to last st, kfb - 13sts
Row 5: Purl
Rows 6-7: Repeat last 2 rows once - 14sts
Row 8: Knit
Row 9: Purl
Row 10: Knit to last 2 sts k2tog - 13sts
Rows 11-14: Repeat last 2 rows twice - 11sts
Row 15: Cast off 5 sts purlwise for right **Foot Top**, purl to end - 6sts
Row 16: Knit

Cast off all 6 sts purlwise for right **Inner Leg**.

Remove **Foot Markers**.

Sewing the Feet

Working on one foot at a time, fold foot in half with WS together (*see fig. 5, straight line*) matching the decreases and increases (*see fig. 5, dotted line to dotted line*) for the top of the foot.

Mattress stitch along the **Foot Top** to the fold, and then mattress stitch along the back of the foot at the ankle. Tuck in yarn ends and stuff the foot though the **Inner Leg** opening.

With yarn **JJ** sew four straight stitches over the paw for the claws.

FRONT AND BELLY

Forelegs

With RS facing you, with yarn **EFG** pick up and knit 8 sts from squirrel's right **Foreleg Marker** (*see fig. 3, C*) to squirrel's right **Neck Marker** (*see fig. 3, D*), backward loop cast on 8 sts, pick up and knit 8 sts from left **Neck Marker** (*see fig. 3, E*) to left **Foreleg Marker** (*see fig. 3, F*) - 24sts

Row 1 (WS): Purl

Row 2: K8, skpo, k4, k2tog, knit to end - 22sts

Row 3: Purl

Row 4: K8, skpo, k2, k2tog, knit to end - 20sts

Rows 5-7: Work 3 rows stocking stitch starting with a purl row

Row 8: Cast off 4 sts, knit to last 4 sts, cast off 4 sts - 12sts

Remove **Foreleg Markers**.

Rejoin yarn **EFG** to remaining 12 sts.

Row 9 (WS): Purl

Row 10: Kfb, knit to last st, kfb - 14sts

Row 11-12: Repeat last 2 rows once - 16sts

Rows 13-15: Work 3 rows stocking stitch starting with a purl row

PM at each end of last row for **Side Seam Markers**.

Row 16: Kfb, knit to last st, kfb - 18sts

Row 17-21: Work 5 rows stocking stitch starting with a purl row

Row 22: [Kfb] 6 times, k6, kfb 6 times - 30sts

PM at each end of last row for **Inner Thigh Markers**.

Row 23: Purl

Row 24: Cast off 12 sts, kfb, k2, kfb, k1, cast off 12 sts - 8sts

Belly

With yarn **BFG** return to the remaining 8 sts.

Rows 25-37: Work 13 rows stocking stitch starting with a purl row

Cut **B** and join **E** to work with **EFG**.

PM at each end of last row for **Belly End Markers**.

Rows 38-43: Work 6 rows stocking stitch

Cut **EF** and join **H** to work with yarn **GH**.

Rows 44-45: Work 2 rows stocking stitch

Cast off.

Note: This cast-off edge will be joined to the base of the tail after the tail is knitted.

TAIL

With yarn **GH** slip the 7 tail sts onto LH needle with RS facing you.

Rows 1-8 (RS): Work 8 rows stocking stitch

Row 9: K1, kfb, k3, kfb, k1 - 9sts

Row 10: Purl

Row 11: K1, kfb, k5, kfb, k1 - 11sts

Row 12: Purl

Row 13: K2, kfb, k5, kfb, knit to end - 13sts

Row 14: Purl

Row 15: K3, kfb, k5, kfb, knit to end - 15sts

Row 16: Purl

Row 17: K3, kfb, k7, kfb, knit to end - 17sts

Row 18: Purl

Row 19: K3, kfb, k9, kfb, knit to end - 19sts

Row 20: Purl

Row 21: K3, kfb, k11, kfb, knit to end - 21sts

Row 22: Purl

Row 23: K3, kfb, k13, kfb, knit to end - 23sts

Row 24: Purl

Row 25: K4, kfb, k13, kfb, knit to end - 25sts

Row 26: Purl

Row 27: K5, skpo, k11, k2tog, knit to end - 23sts

Row 28: Purl

Row 29: K5, skpo, k9, k2tog, knit to end - 21sts

Row 30: Purl

Row 31: K5, skpo, k7, k2tog, knit to end - 19sts

Row 32: Purl

Row 33: K5, skpo, k5, k2tog, knit to end - 17sts

Row 34: Purl

Row 35: K5, skpo, k3, k2tog, knit to end - 15sts

Row 36: Purl

Row 37: K2tog, k3, skpo, k1, k2tog, knit to last 2, k2tog - 11sts

Row 38: Purl

Row 39: K2tog, k1, skpo, k1, k2tog, k1, k2tog - 7sts

Row 40: Purl

Row 41: K2tog, k3, k2tog - 5sts

Row 42: P1, p2tog, p1 - 4sts

Cast off.

Match the start of the tail to the belly cast-off and whip stitch to join.

Note: The tail itself does not require seaming.

NECK AND CHIN

With RS facing you, with yarn **EFG** pick up and knit 10 sts across the cast-on edge from the right **Neck Marker** to the left **Neck Marker**.

Row 1: Purl

Row 2: K2tog, knit to last 2 sts, k2tog - 8sts.

Row 3: Purl

PM at each end of last row for **White Chin Marker**

Row 4: K2, skpo, k2tog, k2 - 6sts

Row 5: Purl

Row 6: K1, skpo, k2tog, k1 - 4sts

Row 7: Purl

Work short rows to shape the tiny chin:

Short row 1: K3, W+T

Short row 2: P2, W+T

Short row 3: K1, W+T

Short row 4: Purl to end

Cut yarn and thread end through all 4 sts, pull up and secure the end.

NOSE

With RS facing you, with yarn **CE** pick up and knit 6 sts across the cast-on edge from the beginning of the pattern.

Row 1: P2tog, p2, p2tog - 4sts

Row 2: Skpo, k2tog - 2sts

Row 3: P2tog

Fasten off.

EARS

Note: Each ear is picked up and knitted inside the ear gaps.

Squirrel's Left Ear Back

With RS facing you, with yarn **D** pick up and knit 6 sts across the cast-on edge at the back of squirrel's left **Ear Space** *(see fig. 6, A to B)*. The first and last of these 6 sts should be picked up in the ends of the cast-off edge at the front.

Rows 1-3: Work 3 rows stocking stitch starting with a purl row

Row 4: Knit to last 2 sts, k2tog - 5sts

Row 5: P2tog, purl to end - 4sts

Row 6: Knit to last 2 sts, k2tog - 3sts

Row 7: K3tog

Fasten off.

Squirrel's Left Ear Inner

With RS facing you, with yarn **EI** pick up and knit 5 sts across the cast-off edge at the front of squirrel's left **Ear Space** *(see fig. 6, C to D)*.

Row 1: P2tog, purl to end - 4sts

Row 2: Knit

Rows 3-4: Repeat last 2 rows once - 3sts

Row 5: P3tog

Fasten off.

Squirrel's Right Ear Back

With RS facing you, with yarn **D** pick up and knit 6 sts across the cast-on edge at the back of squirrel's right **Ear Space**. The first and last of these 6 sts should be picked up in the ends of the cast-off edge at the front.

Rows 1-3: Work 3 rows stocking stitch starting with a purl row

Row 4: K2tog, knit to end - 5sts

Row 5: Purl to last 2 sts, p2tog - 4sts

Row 6: K2tog, knit to end - 3sts

Row 7: P3tog

Fasten off.

Squirrel's Right Ear inner

With RS facing you, with yarn **EI** pick up and knit 5 sts across the cast-off edge at the front of squirrel's right **Ear Space**.

Row 1: Purl to last 2 sts, p2tog - 4sts

Row 2: Knit

Rows 3-4: Repeat last 2 rows once - 3sts

Row 5: P3tog

Fasten off.

Sewing the Ears

Working on one ear at a time join the fastened-off point of the ear inner to the fastened-off point of the ear back, then neatly whip stitch along each side to join the ear inner to the inside of the ear back.

EYES

Make two alike.

With yarn **EI** cast on 2 sts.

Row 1: [Kfb] twice - 4sts

Row 2: Purl

Row 3: Kfb, k2, kfb - 6sts

Row 4: Purl

Row 5: K2tog, knit to last 2 sts, k2tog - 4sts

Row 6: Purl

Row 7: [K2tog] twice - 2sts

Row 8: P2tog

Fasten off.

Sewing the Eyes

Working on one eye at a time slip the knitted eye into the eye space *(see fig. 7)*, and neatly whip stitch around the edges to join. Insert the toy eye into the centre of each eye. Make sure you are happy with the placement before attaching the backing to secure the eyes.

FORELEG FEET

Work both foreleg feet alike.

With RS facing you return to the row ends at the end of the left foreleg, with yarn **AD**, pick up and knit 7 sts across both colours from one corner to the other *(see fig. 8, dotted line A to B)*.

Rows 1-3: Work 3 rows stocking stitch starting with a purl row

Work short rows to shape the paw:

Short row 1: K5, W+T

Short row 2: P3, W+T

Short row 3: K2, W+T

Short row 4: P1, W+T

Short row 5: Knit to end

Rows 4: P2tog, p3tog, p2tog - 3sts

Cut yarn, thread through 3 sts, pull up and secure end.

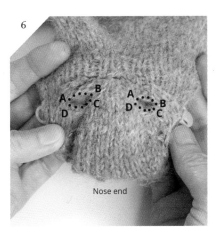

6

Nose end

7

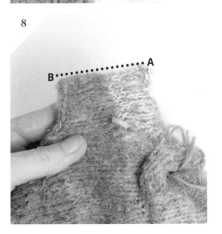

8

SEWING THE BACK TO THE FRONT

Begin at the chin

Working on one side at a time, match the fastened-off tip of the chin to the fastened-off tip of the nose, then match each **Chin Marker** to the **White Chin Marker**. Then mattress stitch from the tip of the chin, past the **Chin Marker**, to the **Neck Marker**.

Note: You will have to ease a little here and there to make the chin fit around the cheeks. Make sure this easing and fitting is symmetrical with both side of the chin.

Remove **Chin**, **White Chin**, and **Neck Markers**.

With yarn **JJ** sew a 'Y' for the nose detail.

Join Hind Legs to Front

Working on one side at a time match the **Thigh Marker** to the **Inner Thigh Marker**, and align the top of the hind leg, with the cast-off edge at the side of the belly. Then align the cast-off edge of the hind leg with the row ends at the side of the belly, matching the end of the hind leg cast-off with the **Belly End Marker** (see fig. 9).

Note: You will need to ease the edges to make the top of the hind leg fit - you want to create that curve at the haunches.

Then mattress stitch to join from the **Thigh Marker** to the **Belly End Marker**.

Remove **Inner Thigh Markers**.

Working on one side at a time match the section between the **Belly End Marker** and the base of the tail with the foot top cast-off edge (see fig. 10, dotted line), and mattress stitch to join.

Remove **Belly End Markers**.

Join Forelegs

Working on one side at a time match the **Side Seam** to the **Side Seam Marker** and align the cast-off edges of the front and back of the forearm. Then mattress stitch from the **Side Seam** up to the foreleg, and then along the foreleg, finally joining all around the feet (see fig. 9, dotted line).

With yarn **JJ** sew four straight stitches over the paw for the claws.

Remove **Side Seam Markers**.

Join Final seams

Working on one side at a time mattress stitch to join front to back from **Side Seam** to **Thigh Marker**.

Tuck in yarn ends and stuff the squirrel before you complete your last seam.

Remove **Thigh Markers**.

Finishing Touch

If desired, work a couple of stitches to join the tail to the back of the neck (about 2.5cm (1in) from the top of the tail so allowing the top of the tail to curl backwards from the neck).

9

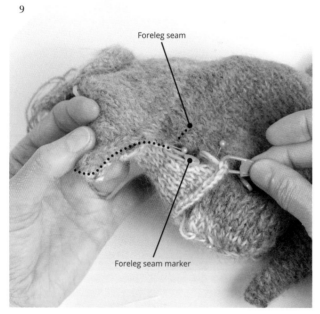

Foreleg seam

Foreleg seam marker

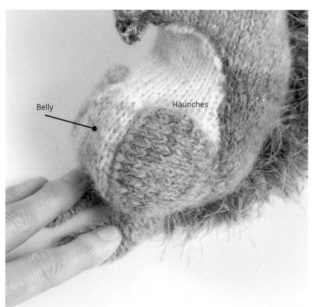

Belly

Haunches

10

Yellow-necked Field Mouse

{Apodemus flavicollis}

———

As you'd imagine the lore surrounding the miniscule mouse is of course all about its size, and yet its size creates the myths associated with its leadership amongst men. Their smallness enables them to succeed at tasks where others have failed, proving that size does not matter as much as courage and persistence.

FINISHED SIZE

Approx. 9cm (3½in) long, excluding tail

YARN

You will need no more than one ball each of:

A: Drops Kid Silk in shade 12 beige

B: Drops Alpaca in shade 2923 goldenrod

C: Drops Flora in shade 02 white

D: Rico Essentials Super Kid Mohair Loves Silk in shade 001 white

E: Drops Alpaca in shade 3112 dusky pink

Unless otherwise stated, multiple strands of yarn are used together throughout this pattern. The exact combinations of yarn to be used are indicated by multiple letters (see How to Use This Book).

NEEDLES

2.5mm knitting needles

TENSION

19 rows and 15 stitches over 5cm (2in) with 2.5mm knitting needles

OTHER TOOLS AND MATERIALS:

· 4 locking stitch markers

· 4mm black safety eyes or tiny black beads

· Toy filling or yarn/fabric scraps

BEGINNING AT THE TAIL END

With yarn **AB** cast on 4 sts.

Row 1 (RS): Kfb, knit to last st, kfb - 6sts
Row 2 (WS): P1, pfb, purl to last 2 sts, pfb, p1 - 8sts
Row 3: Kfb, knit to last st, kfb - 10sts
Row 4: Purl

HIND LEGS

Row 5 (RS): Cast on 7 sts, k7, k2tog, k3, m1, knit to end - 17sts
Row 6 (WS): Cast on 7 sts, p7, p2tog, purl to end - 23sts
Row 7: K11, kfb, knit to end - 24sts
Row 8: Purl
Row 9: Cast off 3 sts for mouse's Right Hind Leg, k8, m1, knit to end - 22sts
Row 10: Cast off 3 sts purlwise for mouse's Left Hind Leg, purl to end - 19sts
Row 11: Skpo, k7, kfb, knit to last 2 sts, k2tog - 18sts
Row 12: P1, p2tog, purl to last 3 sts, p2tog, p1 - 16sts
Row 13: Cast off 3 sts for mouse's Right Thigh, k4, m1, knit to end - 14sts
Row 14: Cast off 3 sts purlwise for mouse's Left Thigh, purl across to end - 11sts
Row 15: Cast on 3 sts for Right Thigh Seam, k8, kfb, knit to end - 15sts
Row 16: Cast on 3 sts for Left Thigh Seam, purl across to end - 18sts
Row 17: Skpo, k5, kfb, k2, kfb, knit to last 2 sts, k2tog
Row 18: Purl
Rows 19-22: Repeat last 2 rows twice

FORELEGS

Work short rows (see General Techniques) to shape mouse's right shoulder:

Short row 1: Cast on 7 sts for mouse's Right Foreleg, k7, k2tog, k3, W+T - 24sts
Short row 2: P5, W+T
Short row 3: K4, W+T
Short row 4: P3, W+T
Short row 5: K2, W+T
Short row 6: Purl to end
Row 23 (RS): Cast off 7 sts, k4, skpo, k2, k2tog, knit to end - 15sts

Work short rows to shape mouse's left shoulder:

Short row 1: Cast on 7 sts for mouse's Left Foreleg, p7, p2tog, p3, W+T - 21sts
Short row 2: K5, W+T
Short row 3: P4, W+T
Short row 4: K3, W+T
Short row 5: P2, W+T
Short row 6: Knit to end
Row 24 (WS): Cast off 7 sts purlwise, p5, p2tog, purl to end - 13sts
Row 25: Skpo, knit to last 2 sts, k2tog - 11sts
Row 26: P4, p3tog, purl to end - 9sts

HEAD

Short rows to create the back of the head:

Short row 1: K8, W+T
Short row 2: P7, W+T
Short row 3: K6, W+T
Short row 4: P5, W+T
Short row 5: K4, W+T
Short row 6: P3, W+T
Short row 7: K2, W+T
Short row 8: P1, W+T
Short row 9: Knit to end
Row 27 (WS): Purl
Row 28: K3, kfb, k1, kfb, knit to end - 11sts
Row 29: Purl
Row 30: Skpo, k2, kfb, k1, kfb, k2, k2tog
Row 31: Purl
Row 32: K4, k3tog, knit to end - 9sts
Row 33: Purl
Row 34: K3, k3tog, knit to end - 7sts
Row 35: Purl
Row 36: K1, skpo, k1, k2tog, k1 - 5sts
Row 37: P1, p3tog, p1 - 3sts

CHIN

Cut **AB** and join on yarn **CD**.
Rows 38-39: Work 2 rows stocking stitch

Row 40 (RS): K1, kfb, k1 - 4sts
Row 41: Purl
Row 42: K1, [kfb] twice, k1 - 6sts
Row 43: Purl
Row 44: K2, [kfb] twice, k2 - 8sts
Row 45: Purl
Row 46: [K2, kfb] twice, k2 - 10sts
Row 47: Purl
Row 48: K3, skpo, k2tog, knit to end - 8sts
Row 49: Purl
Row 50: Kfb, knit to last st, kfb - 10sts
Row 51: Purl
Rows 52-53: Repeat last 2 rows once - 12sts

INNER FORELEGS

Row 54 (RS): Cast on 6 sts for mouse's Right Inner Foreleg, k6, k2tog, knit to end - 17sts
Row 55: Cast on 6 sts for mouse's Left Inner Foreleg, p6, p2tog, purl to end - 22sts
Row 56: Cast off 6 sts, k2, skpo, k2tog, knit to end - 14sts
Row 57: Cast off 6 sts purlwise, purl to end - 8sts

BELLY

Rows 58-63: Work 6 rows stocking stitch
Row 64 (RS): Kfb, k1, skpo, k2tog, k1, kfb
Rows 65-68: Work 4 rows stocking stitch starting with a purl row
PM at each end of last row for **Thigh Markers**.
Row 69: Purl
Row 70: K1, skpo, knit to last 3 sts, k2tog, k1 - 6sts
Row 71: Purl
Row 72: K1, skpo, k2tog, k1 - 4sts
Rows 73-75: Work 3 rows stocking stitch starting with a purl row
PM at each end of last row for **Inner Thigh Markers**.

Row 76: Skpo, k2tog - 2sts
Row 77: Purl

TAIL

Cut **D** and join on **A** so that you're now working with yarn **AC**.

Work 2-stitch i-cord (see General Techniques) until the entire tail measures 9cm (3½in) long

Last row: K2tog.
Fasten off and secure the end. Thread the yarn-ends through the centre and along the length of the i-cord.

RIGHT INNER THIGH

With RS facing you, beginning at the mouse's right **Thigh Marker**, with yarn **CD** pick up and knit 7 sts (see General Techniques) across to the right **Inner Thigh Marker** *(see figs. 1 and 2, A to B)*.

Remove both right **Thigh Markers**.

Rows 1-4: Work 4 rows stocking stitch starting with a purl row
Row 5 (WS): P2tog, purl to last 2 sts, p2tog - 5sts
Rows 6-7: Work 2 rows stocking stitch
Row 8: Skpo, k3 - 4sts
Row 9: Purl
Cast off.

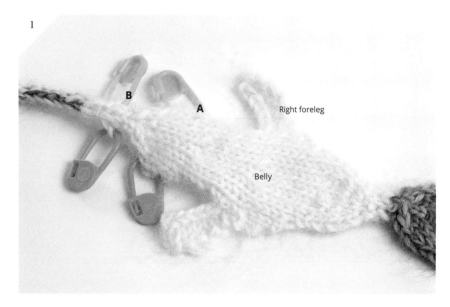

1

B
A
Right foreleg
Belly

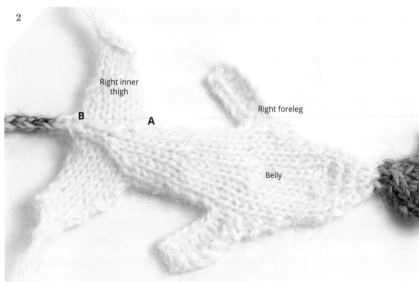

2

Right inner thigh
B
A
Right foreleg
Belly

LEFT INNER THIGH

With RS facing you, beginning at the mouse's left **Inner Thigh Marker**, with yarn **CD** pick up and knit 7 sts across to the left **Thigh Marker**.

Remove both left **Thigh Markers**.

Rows 1-4: Work 4 rows stocking stitch starting with a purl row

Row 5: P2tog, purl to last 2 sts, p2tog - 5sts

Rows 6-7: Work 2 rows stocking stitch

Row 8: K3, k2tog - 4sts

Row 9: Purl

Cast off.

TO MAKE UP

Carefully press the knitting (first checking the yarn manufacturer's guidance about pressing).

With RS together, working on one side at a time, match together then back stitch the cast on and cast-off edges for thigh seam (see fig. 3, join dotted line A to B).

Working with one foreleg at a time, with RS facing you, have the cast-on and cast-off edges for inner and outer forelegs adjacent (see fig. 4, join dotted line A to B), making sure that the row ends at the foot end are level. Mattress stitch the seam that joins along the front of each foreleg.

Then continue to join along the seam from shoulder, across head to chin.

Tuck any yarn ends into the head.

FORELEG FEET

The foreleg feet sts are picked up along the row ends of each foreleg (see fig. 4) as follows:

Working with one foot at a time, with RS facing you, with yarn **E**, pick up and knit 4 sts along the row edge of the foreleg - that is 2 sts either side of the seam you created.

Work 3 rows of 4-stitch i-cord.

Cut yarn and thread up a sewing needle with yarn end, pass through the four 'claw' sts, twice, do not pull up to close the stitches just secure the end and weave it back through the i-cord.

Fold the foreleg and mattress stitch the back seam.

Then mattress stitch the seam that joins the back to the belly from the back foreleg seam along to the thigh seam on the back and where you picked up for the inner thighs on the belly *(see fig. 5)*.

Mould and shape each little foreleg with your fingers to sculpt, shape and bend it a little.

Working with one hind leg at a time, line up the row ends and cast-off edges for inner and outer hind legs *(see fig. 6, join dotted line A to dotted line B)* making sure both sets of row ends at the foot end are level. Mattress stitch the seam that joins along the front of each hind leg.

Tuck any yarn ends into the body.

The hind leg feet sts are picked up along the row ends *(see fig. 6, dotted line)* of each hind leg and worked as follows:

RIGHT HIND FOOT

With RS facing you and with yarn **E**, pick up and knit 6 sts along the row edges of the hind leg - that is 3 sts either side of the seam you created.

Row 1: Purl
Row 2: Skpo, k4, do not turn
Rows 3-6: Work 5-stitch i-cord for 4 rows, do not turn
Row 7: Skpo, k3 - 4sts
Cut yarn and thread end through the four 'claw' sts, thread through all four sts again, do not pull up to close the sts just secure the end and pass it back through the foot i-cord.

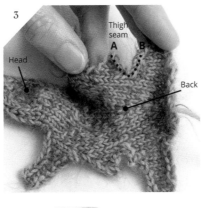

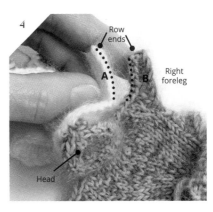

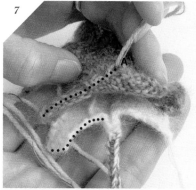

LEFT HIND FOOT

With RS facing you and with yarn **E**, pick up and knit 6 sts along the row edge of the hind leg.

Row 1: Purl

Row 2: K4, k2tog, do not turn

Rows 3-6: Work 5-stitch i-cord for 4 rows, do not turn

Row 7: K3, k2tog - 4sts

Cut yarn and thread end through the four 'claw' sts, thread through all four sts again, do not pull up to close the sts just secure the end and pass it back through the foot i-cord.

Fit the toy eyes in place (or sew on tiny beads), referring to the photographs for placement.

Work 2 tiny stitches in pink yarn across the colour change at the nose for the nose.

Tuck in all remaining yarn ends and stuff the mouse's head and body.

REAR END

Find the centre of the cast-on edge that you began with at the beginning of the pattern *(see fig. 7, A)*.

Match this point with the centre of the base of the tail, then working on one side of the tail at a time, mattress stitch to join along the seam that runs from the tail all along to the hind leg foot.

Note: There is a lot of easing to fit here so take your time.

Mould and shape each little hindleg with your fingers to sculpt, shape and bend it a little.

EARS - MAKE 2 ALIKE

With yarn **AE** cast on 8 sts.

Short row 1: K6, W+T

Short row 2: P4, W+T

Short row 3: K3, W+T

Short row 4: P2, W+T

Short row 5: K1, W+T

Short row 6: P3, W+T

Short row 7: Knit to end

Cut yarn, pass end through the live stitches and pull up to gather, secure the gather and push the ear inside out so that the WS become the inside of the ear.

Note: It's this 'pulled up' edge that is sewn onto the head.

Use the tail ends to join each ear onto the top of the head just after the short row shaping for head back.

Common Pheasant

{Phasianus colchicus}

The mystery and myth surrounding the poor pheasant
does not bode that well. It appears it's much maligned,
in fact in some accounts "The pheasant is a symbol
of ill omen and is believed to turn into an oyster or
a snake during the winter months" but then again,
if it were to turn into an oyster then you may well
reap the rewards of finding a pearl or two!

FINISHED SIZE

Approx. 21cm (8¼in) tall, and 36cm (14in) long from bill tip to tail tip

YARN

You will need no more than one ball each of:

A: Drops Nord in shade 17 plum

B: Drops Alpaca in shade 7240 petrol mix

C: Drops Alpaca in shade 5565 light maroon mix

D: Drops Alpaca in shade 2925 rust mix

E: Drops Kid Silk in shade 15 dark brown

F: Drops Flora in shade 02 white

G: Drops Safran in shade 51 petrol

H: Drops Kid Silk in shade 02 black

I: Drops Alpaca in shade 2923 goldenrod

J: Drops BabyAlpaca Silk in shade 2110 wheat

K: Drops Flora in shade 18 red

Unless otherwise stated, multiple strands of yarn are used together throughout this pattern. The exact combinations of yarn to be used are indicated by multiple letters (see How to Use This Book).

NEEDLES

3.75mm knitting needles, plus 3.25mm for the beak

TENSION

15 rows and 11 stitches over 5cm (2in) with 3.75mm knitting needles

OTHER TOOLS AND MATERIALS

· 1 stitch holder

· 7 locking stitch markers

· 6mm yellow toy safety eyes or glue on eyes

· Toy filling or yarn/fabric scraps

· A pair of wire bird legs, beige florist's tape, and glue to attach the legs (see Tools and Materials)

BEGINNING AT THE BREAST

With yarn **ABC** and 3.75mm needles, cast on 30 sts.

Note: The first section is worked in garter stitch.

Row 1 (WS): K13, kfb, k2, kfb, knit to end - 32sts

Row 2 (RS): Knit

Row 3: K3, kfb, k2, kfb, k18, kfb, k2, kfb, k3 - 36sts

Work short rows (see General Techniques) to shape the left side of the Breast:

Short row 1: K13, W+T

Short row 2: K13

Short row 3: K12, W+T

Short row 4: K12

Short row 5: K11, W+T

Short row 6: K11 - PM at end for **Neck Back Marker**

Short row 7: K10, W+T

Short row 8: K10

Short rows 9-18: Continue as set, working shorter and shorter rows until…

Short row 19: K4, W+T

Short row 20: K4

Row 4 (RS): Knit

Work short rows to shape the right side of the Breast:

Short row 1: K13, W+T

Short row 2: K13

Short row 3: K12, W+T

Short row 4: K12

Short row 5: K11, W+T

Short row 6: K11 - PM at end for **Neck Back Marker**

Short rows 9-18: Continue as set, working shorter and shorter rows until…

Short row 19: K4, W+T

Short row 20: K4

Cut **BC** and join on **D** to work with yarn **AD**.

Row 5 (WS): Knit all sts

Work short rows to shape the Breast Front:

Short row 1: K33, W+T

Short row 2: K30, W+T

Short row 3: K29, W+T

Short row 4: K28, W+T

Short row 5: K27, W+T

Short row 6: K26, W+T

Short row 7: K25, W+T

Short row 8: K24, W+T

Short row 9: K23, W+T

Short row 10: K22, W+T

Short row 11: K21, W+T

Short row 12: K20, W+T

Short row 13: K19, W+T

Short row 14: K18, W+T

Short row 15: K17, W+T

Short row 16: K16, W+T

Short row 17: Knit to end

Row 6 (WS): Knit

The following section is worked in reverse stocking stitch.

Row 7 (RS): Purl

Row 8: Cast off 8 sts, knit to end - 28sts

Row 9: Cast off 8 sts purlwise, purl to end - 20sts

PM at each end of last row for **Wing Markers**

Join on **E** to work with yarn **ADE**

Row 10 (WS): K1, skpo, knit to last 3 sts, k2tog, k1 - 18sts

Row 11 (RS): Purl

Rows 12-17: Repeat last 2 rows three times - 12sts

Work short rows to shape the Rump:

Short row 1: K9, W+T

Short row 2: P6, W+T

Short row 3: K5, W+T

Short row 4: P4, W+T

Short row 5: K3, W+T

Short row 6: P2, W+T

Short row 7: Knit to end

Cut yarns, leave all 12 sts on a stitch holder for later.

NECK AND HEAD

Return to the cast-on edge from the beginning of the pattern, and using yarn **FF** and 3.75mm needles, and with RS facing you, pick up and knit 25 sts (see General Techniques) along this edge.

Note: You will be working the neck and head in stocking stitch.

Row 1 (WS): Purl

Work shorts rows to shape the Collar:

Short row 1: K17, W+T

Short row 2: P9, W+T

Short row 3: Knit to end

Cut **FF** and join on yarn **BG**

Row 2 (WS): Purl

Row 3 (RS): Skpo, knit to last 2 sts, k2tog - 23sts

Row 4: Purl

Work shorts rows to shape the Throat:

Short row 1: K17, W+T

Short row 2: P11, W+T

Short row 3: Knit to end

Row 5 (WS): Purl

Row 6 (RS): Skpo, knit to last 2 sts, k2tog - 21sts

Row 7: Purl

Row 8: Kfb, k7, skpo, k1, k2tog, k7, kfb

Row 9: Purl

Row 10: Kfb, knit to last st, kfb - 23sts

Row 11: Cast off 4 sts purlwise, purl to end - 19sts

Row 12: Cast off 4 sts, join **H** to work with yarn **BGH**, knit to end - 15sts

Row 13: P6, p2tog, PM for **Beak Marker**, purl to end - 14sts

Left Cheek

Work Left Side of head:

Row 14 (RS): Kfb, k6, turn

Row 15 (WS): P8

Row 16: Kfb, k6, kfb - 10 left side sts

Row 17: Purl

Cast off Left Side sts.

Right Cheek

With RS facing you, rejoin yarn **BGH** to remaining 7 sts for Right Side of head:

Row 14 (RS): K6, kfb - 8 sts

Row 15 (WS): Purl

Row 16: Kfb, knit to last st, kfb - 10sts

Row 17: Purl

Cast off Right Side sts.

Matching the row ends, join the neck seam from collar up to the cast-off edges *(see fig. 1)*, using mattress stitch and matching yarn.

Crest

With RS facing you and yarn **BG** pick up and knit 6 sts across cast-off edges *(see fig. 1 dotted lines)* - 3 sts each side of the neck seam.

Rows 1-7: Work 7 rows stocking stitch starting with a purl row

Row 8 (RS): K2, k2tog, k2 - 5sts

Rows 9-15: Work 7 rows stocking stitch starting with a purl row

Row 16 (RS): K1, k3tog, k1 - 3sts

Row 17: Purl

Row 18: K3tog

Fasten off.

Starting at the beak end, ease and mattress stitch the crest along the cast-off edges from the cheeks and along sides down to neck seam to complete the top of the head.

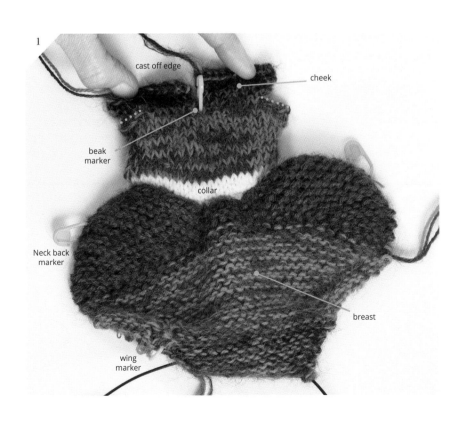

1
cast off edge
cheek
beak marker
collar
Neck back marker
breast
wing marker

NECK BACK

With RS facing you and yarn **DHI** and 3.75mm needles, beginning at the **Neck Back Marker**, pick up and knit 14 sts along to the other **Neck Back Marker** - 7 sts each side of the neck seam.

Work short rows to shape the right Neck Back:

Short row 1: P6, W+T
Short row 2: K6
Short row 3: P5, W+T
Short row 4: K5
Short rows 5-10: Continue as set, working shorter and shorter rows until…
Short row 11: P1, W+T
Short row 12: K1
Cast off 7 sts purlwise, purl to end - 7sts

Work short rows to shape the left Neck Back:

Short row 1: K6, W+T
Short row 2: P6
Short row 3: K5, W+T
Short row 4: P5
Short rows 5-10: Continue as set, working shorter and shorter rows until…
Short row 11: P1, W+T
Short row 12: P1
Cast off.

Mattress stitch the row ends together at the centre back.

BEAK

With yarn **J** and 3.25mm needles cast on 9 sts.

Row 1 (WS): Purl
Row 2 (RS): Kfb, k1, skpo, k1, k2tog, k1, kfb
Row 3: P3, p3tog, p3 - 7sts
Row 4: Kfb, k1, k3tog, k1, kfb
Row 5: P2, p3tog, p2 - 5sts
Row 6: K1, k3tog, k1 - 3sts
Row 7: P3tog
Fasten off.

With WS together, fold beak in half so row ends align and whip stitch to join row ends keeping the tip as pointy as possible. I inserted a rolled up then twisted bit of tissue paper into my beak to help keep its shape.

Tuck in yarn end and stuff the head and neck now.

Remove **Beak Marker** and push the cast-on edge of the beak a little way into the gap at the front of the head.

Stitch carefully in place - a bit fiddly but worth taking the extra time to get it looking as you want it.

RED EYE MARKINGS - MAKE 2 ALIKE

With yarn **K** and 3.25mm needles cast on 7 sts.

Rows 1-6: Work 6 rows stocking stitch
Row 7 (RS): K7 then pick up and knit 3 sts along the row ends (down to tail end at cast-on edge) - 10sts
Row 8: [P2tog] five times - 5sts
Row 9: Skpo, k1, k2tog - 3sts
Cut yarn, thread end through 3 sts.

Pull yarn tail to tighten the sts, stitch this edge (RS facing you) along the seam at the top of the head (see fig. 2, dotted line). Shape then work a couple of stitches to hold in place.

Fit in or glue on the eyes in the centre of the red patches as shown.

RIGHT WING

With RS facing you, working on bird's right side, with yarn **CDK** and 3.75mm needles, pick up and knit 12 sts from **Neck Back Marker** to **Wing Marker**.

Row 1 (WS): Purl
Row 2 (RS): K1, kfb knit to last st, kfb - 14sts
Rows 3-4: Repeat last 2 rows once - 16sts
Row 5: Purl
Row 6: K1, kfb knit to end - 17sts
Rows 7-10: Repeat last 2 rows twice - 19sts

Work short rows to shape the lower edge of the right wing:

Short row 1: P2tog, p8, W+T - 18sts
Short row 2: K9
Short row 3: P2tog, p6, W+T - 17sts
Short row 4: K7
Short row 5: P2tog, p4, W+T - 16sts
Short row 6: K5
Short row 7: P2tog, p2, W+T - 15sts
Short row 8: K3
Cast off all 15 sts purlwise.

Mattress stitch to join the neck back edge with the row ends at the top of the wing (see fig. 3, white dotted line).

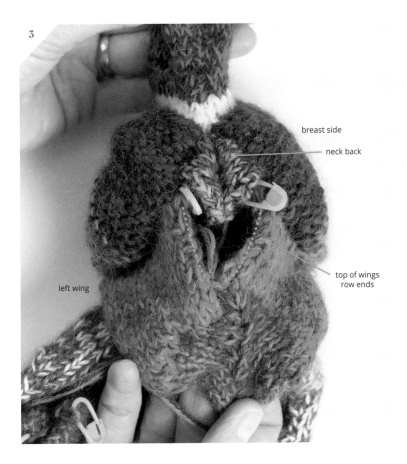

3

breast side

neck back

top of wings
row ends

left wing

LEFT WING

With RS facing you, working on bird's left side, with yarn **CDK** and 3.75mm needles, pick up and knit 12 sts from **Wing Marker** to **Neck Back Marker**.

Row 1 (WS): Purl

Row 2 (RS): Kfb, knit to last 2 sts, kfb, k1 - 14sts

Rows 3-4: Repeat last 2 rows once - 16sts

Row 5: Purl

Row 6: Knit to last 2 sts, kfb, k1 - 17sts

Rows 7-10: Repeat last 2 rows twice - 19sts

Row 11: Purl

Work short rows to shape the lower edge of the left wing:

Short row 1: Skpo, k8, W+T - 18sts

Short row 2: P9

Short row 3: Skpo, k6 W+T - 17sts

Short row 4: P7

Short row 5: Skpo, k4, W+T - 16sts

Short row 6: P5

Short row 7: Skpo, k2, W+T - 15sts

Short row 8: P3

Cast off all 15 sts.

Mattress stitch to join the neck edge with the row ends at the top of the wing - easing it in place because it's slightly wider on this wing *(see fig. 3, yellow dotted line)*.

Remove both **Neck Back Markers**.

LOWER RIGHT WING

With RS facing you, working on bird's right side, with yarn **CEJ** and 3.75mm needles, pick up and knit 11 sts from the tip of the right wing *(see fig. 4)* to **Wing Marker**.

Row 1 (WS): Purl

Row 2: Kfb, knit to end -12sts

Rows 3-4: Repeat last 2 rows once - 13sts

Row 5: Purl

Row 6: Knit to last st, kfb - 14sts

Row 7: Purl

Row 8: Skpo, knit to last 2 sts, k2tog - 12sts

Rows 9-14: Repeat last 2 rows three times - 6sts

Row 15: Purl

Row 16: Kfb, knit to last 2 sts, k2tog

Rows 17-20: Repeat last 2 rows twice

Row 21: P2tog, p4 - 5sts

Cast off.

LOWER LEFT WING

With RS facing you, working on bird's left side, with yarn **CEJ** and 3.75mm needles, pick up and knit 11 sts from the **Wing Marker** to the tip of the left wing.

Row 1 (WS): Purl

Row 2: Knit to last st, kfb - 12sts

Rows 3-4: Repeat last 2 rows once - 13sts

Row 5: Purl

Row 6: Kfb, knit to end - 14sts

Row 7: Purl

Row 8: Skpo, knit to last 2 sts, k2tog - 12sts

Rows 9-14: Repeat last 2 rows three times - 6sts

Row 15: Purl

Row 16: Skpo, knit to last st, kfb

Rows 17-20: Repeat last 2 rows twice

Row 21: Purl to last 2 sts, p2tog - 5sts

Cast off.

Remove **Wing Markers**.

SADDLE

With RS facing you, with yarn **ADE** and 3.75mm needles, pick up and knit 11 sts from the tip of the left wing along to the central seam created at neck back, then pick up and knit 10 sts along to right wing tip - 21sts

Row 1 (WS): P9, p3tog, purl to end - 19sts

Row 2: K7, skpo, k1, k2tog, knit to end - 17sts

Row 3: Purl

Row 4: K7, k3tog, knit to end - 15sts

Row 5: Purl

Row 6: K6, k3tog, knit to end - 13sts

Row 7: Purl

Row 8: K5, k3tog, knit to end - 11sts

Row 9: Purl

Row 10: K4, k3tog, knit to end - 9sts

Row 11: Purl

Row 12: K3, k3tog, knit to end - 7sts

Row 13: Purl

Row 14: K2, k3tog, knit to end - 5sts

Row 15: P2tog, p1, p2tog - 3sts.

Cast off.

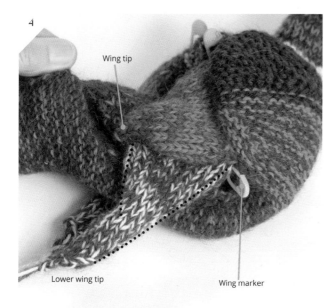

4

Wing tip

Lower wing tip

Wing marker

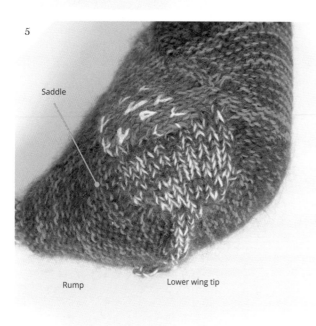

5

Saddle

Rump

Lower wing tip

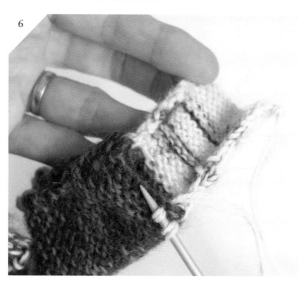

6

RUMP

Slip the 12 rump sts from the stitch holder onto 3.75mm needles ready to work and with RS facing you, join on yarn **ADE**.

Note: You will be working this section in reverse stocking stitch.

Row 1 (RS): Purl

Row 2 (WS): Knit

Rows 3-16: Work 14 rows reverse stocking stitch

Row 17 (RS): Cast on 9 sts, purl to end - 21sts

Row 18 (WS): Cast on 9 sts, knit to end - 30sts

PM at each end of last row for **Tail Marker**.

Row 19: P12, p2tog, p2, p2tog, purl to end - 28sts

Row 20: Knit

Row 21: P11, p2tog, p2, p2tog, purl to end - 26sts

Row 22: Knit

Row 23: P10, p2tog, p2, p2tog, purl to end - 24sts

Row 24: Knit

Row 25: P9, p2tog, p2, p2tog, purl to end - 22sts

Row 26-35: Work 10 rows reverse stocking stitch

Cast off for Tail Opening.

Working on one side at a time, match the **Tail Marker** with the tip of the wing and mattress stitch to join rump row ends to saddle row ends.

Remove **Tail Marker**.

Stitch the rump row ends and cast-on edge *(see fig. 4, dotted lines)* around the lower wing. This will leave you with the tip of the lower wing - about 2.5cm (1in) un-sewn. Fold the wing tip in half at the cast-off edge and join to create a point. Sew the point against the rump *(see fig. 5)*.

Stuff the pheasant's body, tucking in all yarn ends, and taking care to enhance the shaping.

RIGHT TAIL FEATHER

With RS facing you, working on bird's right side, with 3.25mm needles and yarn **EFJ**, beginning at the back seam pick up and knit 9 sts halfway around tail opening *(see fig. 6)*.

Note: In this section you will work stripes of 4 rows in yarn **FJ** and 2 rows in yarn **EFJ**. Carry **E** along the side when not in use.

Row 1: Purl

Row 2: Kfb, knit to last st, kfb - 11sts

Rows 3-4: Repeat last 2 rows once - 13sts

Row 5: Purl

Rows 6-9: With yarn **FJ** work 4 rows stocking stitch

Rows 10-11: With yarn **EFJ** work 2 rows stocking stitch

Rows 12-29: Repeat last 6 rows three times

Row 30: With yarn **FJ** skpo, k3, k3tog, k3, k2tog - 9sts

Rows 31-33: With yarn **FJ** work 3 rows stocking stitch starting with a purl row

Rows 34-35: With yarn **EFJ** work 2 rows stocking stitch

Rows 36-41: Repeat rows 6-11 once

Cut **E** and continue with yarn **FJ**:

Row 42: Skpo, k1, k3tog, k1, k2tog - 5sts

Rows 43-45: Work 3 rows stocking stitch

Cast off.

LEFT TAIL FEATHER

With RS facing you, working on bird's left side, with 3.25mm needles and yarn **EFJ**, beginning halfway around tail opening - where the right tail feather ends - pick up and knit 9 sts around the other half of the tail opening to the back seam *(see fig. 6)*.

Rows 1-42: Work as for right tail feathers Rows 1-42

Rows 43-49: Work 7 rows stocking stitch

Cast off.

Working on one tail feather at a time, flatten the tail feather as best as you can then mattress stitch to join along the row ends - if you wish add wire along the tail feather length or stiffen with starch or similar - mine weren't stuffed but they do have wire in them. Join both tail feathers, top and bottom for about 2.5cm (1in) from the body end.

LEGS

If using, wrap the florist's tape around the wire legs then push the wire legs into the body and glue in place using glue recommended by the manufacturer. If you don't want to use wire legs you could always add lengths of yarn for the legs to tie over a branch as for the Robin.

FACE

To make the face squish up a little, fold a length of yarn in half and pass the cut ends through a yarn sewing needle. Pass the threaded needle through one side of the head, just behind the eye, and out the other side of the head, just behind the eye. Then pass the needle back through the head to emerge back out where you started and through the loop of the folded yarn. Pull up to squish the face and secure the thread.

MARKINGS

Using yarn **J** work simple embroidery stitches for the feather detailing on the wings as follows:

With yarn secured on WS, bring needle out at A, in at B, out at C and over the loop created via A to B, in at D - secure the end *(see fig. 7)*.

Roe Deer Fawn

{Capreolus capreolus}

The woodland goddess Diana was likened to
a deer because of its perceived gracefulness
and swiftness through the forest although
more often the creature be the hunted not
the hunter… still, with a flash of that white
rump (Roe deer don't have a 'tail') they are
quite adept at out pacing their pursuer.

FINISHED SIZE

Approx. 36cm (14in) tall, and 36cm (14in) long

YARN

You will need no more than one ball of each colour, except the rust 4ply - you'll need two of that:

A: Drops Flora in shade 08 brown mix

B: Drops Alpaca in shade 0601 dark brown

C: Drops Alpaca in shade 2915 orange

D: Drops Alpaca in shade 2925 rust mix

E: Drops BabyAlpaca Silk in shade 2110 wheat

F: Drops Flora in shade 02 white

G: Drops Kid Silk in shade 15 dark brown

H: Drops Alpaca in shade 0100 off white

I: Drops Kid Silk in shade 01 off white

Unless otherwise stated, multiple strands of yarn are used together throughout this pattern. The exact combinations of yarn to be used are indicated by multiple letters (see How to Use This Book).

NEEDLES

3.5mm and 3.75mm knitting needles

TENSION

15 rows and 11 stitches over 5cm (2in) with 3.75mm knitting needles

OTHER TOOLS AND MATERIALS

· 1 stitch holder and 2 large safety pins for holding stitches

· 16 locking stitch markers

· 24mm brown or black toy safety eyes

· Toy filling or yarn/fabric scraps

· A small amount of rust coloured felt for the eye, matching thread and a sewing needle

BEGINNING WITH THE NOSE

With yarn **AB** and 3.5mm needles cast on 13 sts.

Row 1 (WS): Purl
Row 2: [K2, kfb] twice, k1, [kfb, k2] twice - 17sts
Row 3: Purl

Work short rows (see General Techniques) to create deer's left side of nose:

Short row 1: Kfb, k1, kfb, k3, W+T - 19sts
Short row 2: P8
Short row 3: K7, W+T
Short row 4: P7
Short row 5: K6, W+T
Short row 6: P6
Short row 7: K3, W+T
Short row 8: P3
Short row 9: K1, W+T
Short row 10: P1

Row 4: K16, kfb, k1, kfb - 21sts

Work short rows to create deer's right side of nose:

Short row 1: P8, W+T
Short row 2: K8
Short row 3: P7, W+T
Short row 4: K7
Short row 5: P6, W+T
Short row 6: K6
Short row 7: P3, W+T
Short row 8: K3
Short row 9: P1, W+T
Short row 10: K1

Row 5: Purl

Cut **B** and join on **C** to work with yarn **AC**.

Row 6: Kfb, knit to last st, kfb - 23sts
Row 7: Purl
Row 8-9: Repeat last 2 rows once - 25sts
Row 10: K16, turn work so WS is facing you
Row 11: P7, turn work so RS is facing you

After working three or four more rows of the nose slip each set of 9 cheek sts onto safety pins.

NOSE

Working on just the 7 nose sts:

Row 12-15: Work 4 rows stocking stitch
Row 16: Kfb, k5, kfb - 9sts
Row 17: P9

Cut **A** and join **D** to work with yarn **CD**:

Row 18: Kfb, k7, kfb - 11sts

PM at each end of last row for **Nose Markers**.

Row 19: Purl
Row 20: Kfb, k9, kfb -13sts
Row 21: Purl
Row 22: Kfb, k11, kfb -15sts
Rows 23-31: Work 9 rows stocking stitch starting with a purl row
Row 32: Kfb, knit to last st, kfb -17sts
Rows 33-35: Work 3 rows stocking stitch starting with a purl row

Row 36: Kfb, knit to last st, kfb -19sts

Rows 37-39: Work 3 rows stocking stitch starting with a purl row

PM at each end of last row for **Head Back Markers.**

Cut the yarns and leave all 19 sts on a stitch holder.

RIGHT SIDE OF NOSE

With RS facing you, slip the 9 sts for deer's right side off the safety pin and onto a 3.5mm knitting needle ready to knit across, rejoin yarn **CD**.

Row 1 (RS): K9

Row 2: Purl

Row 3: Kfb, k8 - 10sts

Row 4: Purl

PM at end of last row for **Eye Corner Marker.**

Row 5: Kfb, k9 - 11sts

Row 6: Purl

Row 7: Kfb, knit to last st, kfb - 13sts

Row 8 Purl

Rows 9-12: Repeat last 2 rows twice - 17sts

Row 13: Kfb, knit to end- 18sts

Row 14: Purl

Rows 15-20: Repeat last two rows three times - 21sts

Rows 21-26: Work 6 rows stocking stitch

PM at end of last row for **Eye Socket Marker.**

Row 27: Cast off 10 sts for **Head Back**, knit to end - 11sts

PM at end of last row for **Neck Marker.**

Work short rows to shape the right side of head:

Short row 1: P10, W+T

Short row 2: K10

Short row 3: P9, W+T

Short row 4: K9

Short row 5-8: Continue as set, working shorter rows each time until…

Short row 9: P6, W+T

Short row 10: K6

PM at end of last row for **Head Seam marker.**

Cast off 11 Head Seam sts purlwise. Leave long tail ends to sew the head back seam.

LEFT SIDE OF NOSE

With WS facing you, slip the 9 sts for deer's left side off the safety pin and onto a 3.5mm knitting needle ready to purl across, rejoin yarn **CD**.

Row 1 (WS): P9

Row 2: K8, kfb - 10sts

Row 3: Purl

Row 4: K9, kfb - 11sts.

PM at end of row for **Eye Corner Marker.**

Row 5: Purl

Row 6: Kfb, k to last st, kfb - 13sts

Row 7: Purl

Rows 8-11: Repeat last 2 rows twice - 17sts

Row 12: Knit to last st, kfb - 18sts

Row 13: Purl

Rows 14-19: Repeat last two rows three times - 21sts

Rows 20-26: Work 7 rows stocking stitch

PM at end of last row for **Eye Socket Marker.**

Row 27: Cast off 10 sts purlwise for **Head Back**, purl to end - 11sts

PM at end of last row for **Neck Marker.**

Work short rows to shape the left side:

Short row 1: K10, W+T

Short row 2: P10

Short row 3: K9, W+T

Short row 4: P9

Short row 5-10: Continue as set, working shorter rows each time until…

Short row 9: K6, W+T

Short row 10: P6

PM at end of last row for **Head Seam Marker.**

Cast off 11 Head Seam sts. Leave long tail ends to sew the head back seam.

LEFT EYE SOCKET

With yarn **EF** and 3.5mm needles, with RS facing you pick up and knit 12 sts (see General Techniques) between the **Eye Socket Marker** and the **Eye Corner Marker** (*see fig. 1, A to B*), then matching the **Eye Corner Marker** to the **Nose Marker**, pick up and knit 10 sts between the **Nose Marker** and the **Head Back Marker** (*see fig. 1, B to C*) - 22sts

Remove **Eye Socket Marker** and **Head Back Marker.**

Row 1 (WS): Purl

Work short rows to shape the bottom of the eye socket:

Short row 1: K10, W+T

Short row 2: P7, W+T

Short row 3: K6, W+T

Short row 4: P5, W+T

Short row 5: K4, W+T

Short row 6: P3, W+T

Short row 7: K2, W+T

Short row 8: Purl to end of row

Row 2: Cast off 13 sts, knit to end - 9sts

Work short rows to shape the eye lid:

Short row 1: P8, W+T

Short row 2: K7, W+T

Short row 3: P6, W+T

Short row 4: K5, W+T

Short row 5: P4, W+T

Short row 6: Knit to end of row

Cast off purlwise. Leave long tail ends to sew the seam.

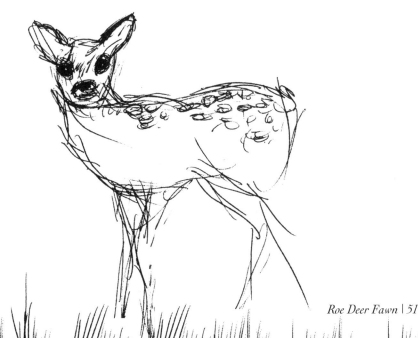

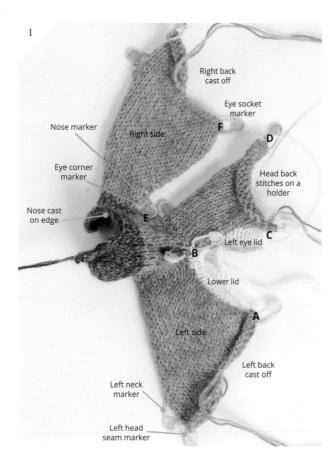

1

Right back cast off

Eye socket marker

Nose marker

Right side

F

D

Eye corner marker

Head back stitches on a holder

Nose cast on edge

E

B

C

Left eye lid

Lower lid

Left side

A

Left back cast off

Left neck marker

Left head seam marker

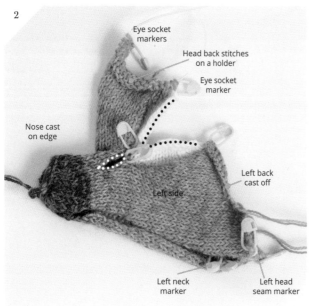

2

Eye socket markers

Head back stitches on a holder

Eye socket marker

Nose cast on edge

Left back cast off

Left side

Left neck marker

Left head seam marker

RIGHT EYE SOCKET

With yarn **EF** and 3.5mm needles, with RS facing you pick up and knit 10 sts between the **Head Back Marker** and the **Nose Marker** (*see fig. 1, D to E*), then matching the **Nose Marker** to the **Eye Corner Marker**, pick up and knit 12 sts between the **Eye Corner Marker** and the **Eye Socket Marker** (*see fig. 1, E to F*) - 22sts.

Remove **Eye Socket Marker** and **Head Back Marker**.

Row 1 (WS): Purl

Work short rows to shape the eye lid:

Short row 1: K8, W+T
Short row 2: P7, W+T
Short row 3: K6, W+T
Short row 4: P5, W+T
Short row 5: K4, W+T
Short row 6: P6 to end of row
Row 2: Cast off 9 sts, knit to end - 13sts

Work short rows to shape the bottom of the eye socket:

Short row 1: P10, W+T
Short row 2: K7, W+T
Short row 3: P6, W+T
Short row 4: K5, W+T
Short row 5: P4, W+T
Short row 6: K3, W+T
Short row 7: P2, W+T
Short row 8: K7 to end of row

Cast off purlwise. Leave long tail ends to sew the seam.

SEWING THE NOSE

With RS together, fold nose in half across cast-on edge and back stitch along cast-on edge only. Working on one side at a time, match the **Nose Marker** with the **Eye Corner Marker** with RS together (*see fig. 2, white dotted line*), and back stitch to join.

Remove **Nose Markers** and **Eye Corner Markers**.

Working on one eye at a time, fold the eye so that the cast-off edges from bottom of the eye and eye lid are matching with RS together (*see fig. 2, black dotted line*), then back stitch the edges together.

HEAD BACK

With yarn **CD** and 3.5mm needles, with RS facing you pick up and knit 9 sts along the **Left Head Back** cast-off edge, slip the 19 head back sts from the holder onto a needle and knit across them, then pick up and knit 9 sts along the **Right Head Back** cast-off edge (*see fig. 3, X to Y*) - 37sts

Row 1 (WS): Purl, pull tension taut as you purl across the joins

Row 2: K7, skpo, k2tog, k15, skpo, k2tog, knit to end - 33sts
Rows 3, 5, 7, 9, 11: Purl
Row 4: K7, skpo, k15, k2tog, knit to end - 31sts
Row 6: K6, skpo, k15, k2tog, knit to end - 29sts
Row 8: K5, skpo, k15, k2tog, knit to end - 27sts
Row 10: K4, skpo, k15, k2tog, knit to end - 25sts
Row 12: K3, skpo, k15, k2tog, knit to end - 23sts
Row 13: Purl

PM at each end of last row for **Head Seam Marker**.

NECK

Row 14: Cast on 9 sts for neck, knit to end of the row - 32sts

Row 15: Cast on 9 sts neck, purl to end of the row - 41sts

Row 16: Kfb, k16, skpo, k3, k2tog, k16, kfb.

PM at each end of last row for **Neck Marker**

Row 17: Purl

Rows 18-39: Repeat last 2 rows eleven times

Stop the knitting here, but do not cut yarn.

Working on one side at a time, match **Head Seam Markers** and mattress stitch to join the cast-off edge with the head back row ends *(see fig. 4, dotted line)*. There's quite a bit of easing here so you may wish to pin or tack first.

Remove the **Head Seam Markers**.

Working on one side at a time, match **Neck Marker** and mattress stitch to join the row ends from the cast-on edge *(see fig. 4, A and B)*.

Keep one **Neck Marker** from each side of the head in place for now, you'll need them when you join the chin later.

BACK AND RUMP

Switch to 3.75mm needles and join on **G** to work with yarn **CDG**.

Row 25 (RS): K20, kfb, knit to end - 42sts

Rows 26, 28, 30, 32: Purl

Row 27: K19, kfb, k2, kfb, knit to end - 44sts

Row 29: K19, kfb, k2, m1, k2, kfb, knit to end - 47sts

Row 31: K19, kfb, k3, kfb, k3, kfb, knit to end - 50sts

Row 33: K19, kfb, k5, m1, k5, kfb, knit to end - 53sts

PM at each end of last row for **Foreleg Position Markers**.

Row 34: Purl

Row 35: K19, kfb, k6, kfb, k6, kfb, knit to end - 56sts

Row 36: Purl

Row 37: K19, kfb, k8, m1, k8, kfb, knit to end - 59sts

Rows 38-40: Work 3 rows stocking stitch starting with a purl row

PM at each end of last row for **Foreleg Position Markers**.

Rows 41-64: Work 24 rows stocking stitch

Row 65: K18, skpo, k8, k3tog, k8, k2tog, knit to end - 55sts

Rows 66, 68, 70, 72 74: Purl

Row 67: K18, skpo, k6, k3tog, k6, k2tog, knit to end - 51sts

PM at each end of last row for **Belly Markers**.

Row 69: K18, skpo, k4, k3tog, k4, k2tog, knit to end - 47sts

Row 71: K18, skpo, k2, k3tog, k2, k2tog, knit to end - 43sts

Row 73: K20, k3tog, knit to end - 41sts

Row 75: K19, k3tog, knit to end - 39sts

Row 76: Cast off 11 sts purlwise for **Rump End**, p16 (tail sts), cast off last 11 sts purlwise for **Rump End** - 17sts

Cut yarns.

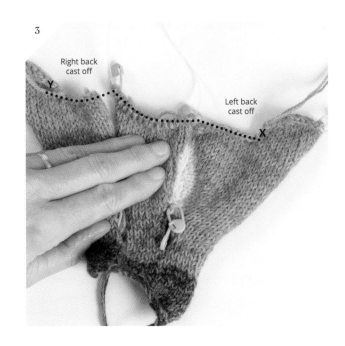

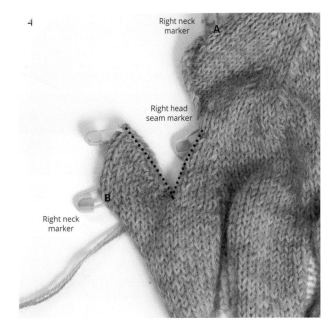

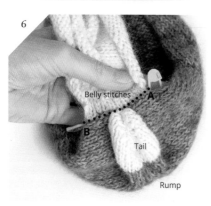

6

Belly stitches A

B

Tail

Rump

7

A

B

TAIL

Join yarn **FHI**.

Row 1: Knit

Work short rows to shape the tail right side:

Short row 1: P8 W+T

Short row 2: K8

Short row 3: P7, W+T

Short row 4: K7

Short rows 5-12: Continue as set, working shorter rows each time until…

Short row 13: P2, W+T

Short row 14: K2

Row 2: Purl

Work short rows to shape the tail left side:

Short row 1: K8 W+T

Short row 2: P8

Short row 3: K7, W+T

Short row 4: P7

Short rows 5-12: Continue as set, working shorter rows each time until…

Short row 13: K2, W+T

Short row 14: P2

Cast off all sts.

With RS together, match both **Rump End** cast-off edges and back stitch to join.

With RS together, fold tail in half across cast-off edge and back stitch along cast-off edge only.

Turn tail RS out and push the tail through to the outside of the body.

Stuff tail with yarn ends and a little stuffing.

Lay the row end from the tail down onto the rump end seam and whip stitch neatly around the tail row ends to attach to the rump as shown *(see fig. 5)*.

BELLY

With yarn **FHI** and with 3.75mm needles, with RS facing you, pick up and knit 10 sts between the two **Belly Markers** (see fig. 6, A to B, dotted line).

Remove **Belly Markers**.

Row 1 (WS): Purl

Row 2: Cast on 40 sts, knit to end - 50sts

Row 3: Cast on 40 sts, purl to end - 90sts

Work short rows for left side of belly:

Short row 1: K44, W+T

Short row 2: P44

Short row 3: K43, W+T

Short row 4: P44

Short row 5: K42, W+T

Short rows 6-12: Continue as set, working shorter rows each time until…

Short row 13: K38, W+T

Short row 14: P38

Row 4: Cast off 45 sts, knit to end - 45sts

Work short rows for right side of belly:

Short row 1: P44 W+T

Short row 2: K44

Short row 3: P43, W+T

Short row 4: K43

Short rows 5-12: Continue as set, working shorter rows each time until…

Short row 13: P38, W+T

Short row 14: K38

Cast off.

Place the left-side and right-side cast-off edges of belly together and mattress stitch to join along cast-off edges. This creates a centre seam along the length of the belly.

JOIN BACK TO UNDERSIDE

Working on one side at a time join the belly to the rump and back.

Begin at the tail end and match the cast-on edges of the belly together with the row ends of the back and neck up to the **Neck Markers** easing them to fit. You may wish to pin in place and tack in place before sewing because it's a long seam.

You can begin to stuff the fawn from here if you wish, so you see the shape that's forming.

THROAT

With yarn **FHI** and 3.5mm needles, with RS facing you, pick up and knit 16 sts between the two **Neck Markers**, picking up 8 sts each side of the belly centre seam *(see fig. 7, A to B dotted line)*.

Remove **Neck Markers**.

Row 1 (WS): Purl

Row 2: K1, kfb, knit to last 2 sts, kfb, k1 - 18sts

Rows 3-6: Repeat last 2 rows twice - 22sts

Row 7: Purl

Row 8: K7, kfb, k6, kfb, knit to end - 24sts

Row 9: Purl

Row 10: Skpo, k6, kfb, k6, kfb, knit to last 2 sts, k2tog

Row 11: Purl

Rows 12-13: Repeat last 2 rows once

Row 14: Skpo, k1, k2tog, knit to last 5 sts, skpo, k1, k2tog - 20sts

Row 15: Purl

Rows 16-19: Repeat last 2 rows twice - 12sts

Row 20: K5, k2tog, knit to end - 11sts

Row 21: Purl

MOUTH

Cut yarn and join on yarn **AB**.

Rows 22-30: Work 9 rows stocking stitch
PM at each end of last row for **Mouth Markers**

Rows 31-39: Work 9 rows stocking stitch starting with a purl row
Cast off.

With RS together, fold the mouth at the **Mouth Markers** so that the cast-off edge matches the beginning of the mouth at the colour change. Back stitch along both sides of row ends then turn RS out.

Place the mouth beneath the nose, matching the row ends from the nose with the sewn edges of the mouth *(see fig. 8)*, and carefully and neatly whip stitch to join to nose to mouth.

Note: You may find it easier to join the mouth to the nose with the head stuffed first.

EYES

Trace the eye template *(see fig. 9)* and cut two in the rust coloured felt. Using sharp scissors, carefully make a hole in the centre of the felt shape before inserting the toy eye.

Working on one eye at a time, position the eye and felt shape into the eye socket seam and fasten into place. With the sewing needle and matching sewing thread use a running stitch to sew the felt shape onto the eye socket as shown.

Complete the seam that joins both sides of the head to the chin by matching the row ends and mattress stitching, adding more stuffing if necessary.

RIGHT FORELEG

With yarn **CD** and 3.5mm needles cast on 19 sts.

Rows 1-34: Work 34 rows stocking stitch

Right Foreleg Knee Joint

Row 35 (RS): K10, [kfb, k1] four times, k1 - 23sts

Row 36: Purl

Row 37: K10, [kfb, k2] 4 times, k1 - 27sts

Row 38: Purl

Row 39: K10, [kfb, k3] 4 times, k1 - 31sts

Rows 40-42: Work 3 rows stocking stitch starting with a purl row

Row 43: K10, [k2tog, k3] 4 times, k1 - 27sts

Row 44: Purl

Row 45: K10, [k2tog, k2] 4 times, k1 - 23sts

Row 46: Purl

Row 47: K10, [k2tog, k1] 4 times, k1 - 19sts

Row 48: P10, [p2tog, p1] 3 times - 16sts

Rows 49-70: Work 22 rows stocking stitch

Row 71: K1, kfb, knit to last 2 sts, kfb, k1 - 18sts

Row 72: Purl

Rows 73-74: Repeat last 2 rows once - 20sts

The stitches are now divided to work the hoof in three sections.

Right Foreleg Hoof section 1 (front outside)

Work this section on just the first 6 sts:

Row 75 (RS): K1, kfb, k4 - 7sts

Row 76: Purl

Cut **CD** and join on yarn **AA**.

Row 77-82: Work 6 rows stocking stitch

Row 83: K1, k2tog, knit to end - 6sts

Row 84: Purl

Rows 85-88: Repeat last 2 rows twice - 4sts

Cast off.

Right Foreleg Hoof section 2 (front inside)

Rejoin yarn **CD** to work this section on the next 6 sts:

Row 75 (RS): K4, kfb, k1 - 7sts

Row 76: Purl

Cut **CD** and join on yarn **AA**.

Row 77-82: Work 6 rows stocking stitch

Row 83: Knit to last 3 sts, k2tog, k1 - 6sts

Row 84: Purl

Rows 85-88: Repeat last 2 rows twice - 4sts

Cast off.

Right Foreleg Hoof section 3 (back)

Rejoin yarn **CD** to work this section on the last 8 sts:

Row 75 (RS): K1, kfb, k4, kfb, k1 - 10sts

Row 76: Purl

Cut **CD** and join on yarn **AA**.

Row 77-82: Work 6 rows stocking stitch

Row 83: K1, skpo, knit to last 3 sts, k2tog, k1 - 8sts

Row 84: Purl

Rows 85-88: Repeat last 2 rows twice - 4sts

Cast off.

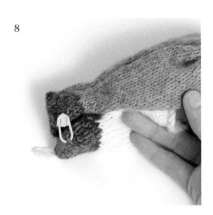

8

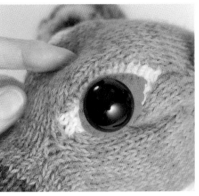

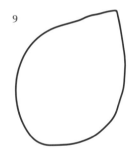

9

LEFT FORELEG

With yarn **CD** and 3.5mm needles cast on 19 sts.

Rows 1-34: Work 34 rows stocking stitch

Left Foreleg Knee Joint

Row 35 (RS): K2, [kfb, k1] 4 times, knit to end - 23sts

Row 36: Purl

Row 37: K2, [kfb, k2] 4 times, knit to end - 27sts

Row 38: Purl

Row 39: K2, [kfb, k3] 4 times, knit to end - 31sts

Rows 40-42: Work 3 rows stocking stitch starting with a purl row

Row 43: K4, k2tog, [k3, k2tog] 3 times, knit to end - 27sts

Row 44: Purl

Row 45: K3, k2tog, [k2, k2tog] 3 times, k to end - 23sts

Row 46: Purl

Row 47: K2, k2tog, [k1, k2tog] 3 times, k to end - 19sts

Row 48: [P1, p2tog] 3 times, p to end - 16sts

Rows 49-70: Work 22 rows stocking stitch

Row 71: K1, kfb, knit to last 2 sts, kfb, k1 - 18sts

Row 72: Purl

Rows 73-74: Repeat last 2 rows once - 20sts

The stitches are now divided to work the hoof in three sections.

Left Foreleg Hoof section 1 (back)

Work this section on just the first 8 sts:

Row 75 (RS): K1, kfb, k4, kfb, k1 - 10sts

Row 76: Purl

Cut **CD** and join on yarn **AA**.

Row 77-82: Work 6 rows stocking stitch

Row 83: K1, skpo, knit to last 3 sts, k2tog, k1 - 8sts

Row 84: Purl

Rows 85-88: Repeat last 2 rows twice - 4sts

Cast off.

Left Foreleg Hoof section 2 (front inside)

Rejoin yarn **CD** to work this section on the next 6 sts:

Row 75 (RS): K1, kfb, k4 - 7sts

Row 76: Purl

Cut **CD** and join on yarn **AA**.

Row 77-82: Work 6 rows stocking stitch

Row 83: K1, k2tog, knit to end - 6sts

Row 84: Purl

Rows 85-88: Repeat last 2 rows twice - 4sts

Cast off.

Left Foreleg Hoof section 3 (front outside)

Rejoin yarn **CD** to work this section on the last 6 sts:

Row 75 (RS): K4, kfb, k1 - 7sts

Row 76: Purl

Cut **CD** and join on yarn **AA**.

Rows 77-82: Work 6 rows stocking stitch

Row 83: Knit to last 3 sts, k2tog, k1 - 6sts

Row 84: Purl

Rows 85-88: Repeat last 2 rows twice - 4sts

Cast off.

Working on one leg at a time, match the hoof fronts with RS together, and back stitch from the top of the hoof to the pointed bottom (*see fig. 10, dotted lines*). Then complete both side seams of the hoof in the same way. Turn out to RS.

Mattress stitch the seam from the hoof to the top, matching row ends, and carefully stuffing fairly firmly but not so as to distort the stitches, as you join.

Tuck the cast-on edge inside a little and sew a running stitch around the top, pull up to close.

Working on one side at a time, position the leg onto the body and belly in between the **Foreleg Position Markers**. Whip stitch around the top of the leg to join leg to body.

RIGHT HIND LEG

With yarn **ACG** and 3.75mm needles cast on 10 sts for **Hind Leg Thigh**.

Row 1: K1, kfb, knit to last 2 sts, kfb, k1 - 12sts

Row 2: Purl

Rows 3-10: Repeat last 2 rows four times - 20sts

Row 11: Cast on 20 sts for **Back of Hind Leg**, knit to end - 40sts

Rows 12, 14, 16, 18, 20, 22, 24, 26, 28, 30, 32, 34: Purl

Row 13: K18, skpo, k2tog, knit to end - 38sts

Row 15: Kfb, k15, skpo, k2, k2tog, knit to last st, kfb

Row 17: Kfb, k15, skpo, k2, k2tog, knit to last st, kfb

Row 19: Kfb, k6, k2tog, k7, skpo, k2, k2tog, k7, k2tog, knit to last st, kfb - 36sts

Row 21: Kfb, k6, k2tog, k6, skpo, k2, k2tog, k6, k2tog, knit to last st, kfb - 34sts

Row 23: Kfb, k6, k2tog, k5, skpo, k2, k2tog, k5, k2tog, knit to last st, kfb - 32sts

Row 25: Kfb, k6, k2tog, k4, skpo, k2, k2tog, k4, k2tog, knit to last st, kfb - 30sts

Row 27: Kfb, k6, k2tog, k3, skpo, k2, k2tog, k3, k2tog, knit to last st, kfb - 28sts

Row 29: Kfb, k6, k2tog, k2, skpo, k2, k2tog, k2, k2tog, knit to last st, kfb - 26sts

Row 31: Kfb, k6, k2tog, k1, skpo, k2, k2tog, k1, k2tog, knit to last st, kfb - 24sts

Row 33: Kfb, k6, k2tog, skpo, k2, [k2tog] twice, k6, kfb - 22sts

Right Hind Leg Joint

Row 35 (RS): K11, m1, knit to end - 23sts
Row 36: Purl
Row 37: K10, [kfb, k2] 4 times, k1 - 27sts
Row 38: Purl
Row 39: K10, [kfb, k3] 4 times, k1 - 31sts
Rows 40-42: Work 3 rows stocking stitch
Row 43: K10, [k2tog, k3] 4 times, k1 - 27sts
Row 44: Purl
Row 45: K10, [k2tog, k2] 4 times, k1 - 23sts
Row 46: Purl
Row 47: K10, [k2tog, k1] 4 times, k1 - 19sts
Rows 48-49: Work 2 rows stocking stitch
Row 50: [P1, p2tog] 3 times, purl to end - 16sts
Rows 51-70: Work 20 rows stocking stitch
Row 71: K1, kfb, knit to last 2 sts, kfb, k1 - 18sts
Row 72: Purl
Rows 73-74: Repeat last 2 rows once - 20sts
The stitches are now divided to work the hoof in two sections.

Right Hind Leg Hoof section 1

Work this section on the first 10 stitches:
Row 75 (RS): K1, kfb, k8 - 11sts
Row 76: Purl
Cut **ACG** and join on yarn **AA**.
Rows 77-82: Work 6 rows stocking stitch
Row 83: K1, k2tog, knit to end - 10sts
Row 84: Purl
Rows 85-86: Repeat last 2 rows - 9sts
Row 87: K1, skpo, k3, k2tog - 7sts
Row 88: Purl
Cast off.

Right Hind Leg Hoof section 2

Rejoin yarn **ACG** to work this section on the remaining 10 sts:
Row 75 (RS): K8, kfb, k1 - 11sts
Row 76: Purl
Cut **ACG** and join on yarn **AA**.
Rows 77-82: Work 6 rows stocking stitch
Row 83: Knit to 3 sts before end, k2tog, k1 - 10sts
Row 84: Purl
Rows 85-86: Repeat last 2 rows - 9sts
Row 87: Skpo, k4, k2tog, k1 - 7sts
Row 88: Purl
Cast off.

LEFT HIND LEG

Rows 1-10: Work as for **Right Hind Leg Rows 1-10**

Row 11: K20, turn, cast on 20 sts for **Back of Hind Leg** - 40sts

Rows 12-34: Work as for **Right Hind Leg Rows 12-34**

Left Hind Leg Joint

Row 35 (RS): K11, m1, knit to end - 23sts

Row 36: Purl

Row 37: K3, [kfb, k2] 4 times, knit to end - 27sts

Row 38: Purl

Row 39: K4, [kfb, k3] 4 times, knit to end - 31sts

Rows 40-42: Work 3 rows stocking stitch

Row 43: K4, k2tog, [k3, k2tog] 3 times, knit to end - 27sts

Row 44: Purl

Row 45: K3, k2tog, [k2, k2tog] 3 times, knit to end - 23sts

Row 46: Purl

Row 47: K2, k2tog, [k1, k2tog] 3 times, knit to end - 19sts

Rows 48-49: Work 2 rows stocking stitch

Row 50: P10, [p2tog, p1] 3 times - 16sts

Rows 51-70: Work 20 rows stocking stitch

Row 71: K1, kfb, knit to last 2 sts, kfb, k1 - 18sts

Row 72: Purl

Rows 73-74: Repeat last 2 rows once - 20sts

Left Hind Leg Hoof section 1

Work as for **Right Hind Leg Hoof section 1**.

Left Hind Leg Hoof section 2

Work as for **Right Hind Leg Hoof section 2**.

Working on one leg at a time, match the hoof sections with WS together, and back stitch all around. Turn out to RS.

Mattress stitch the seam from the hoof to the top, matching row ends, and carefully stuffing fairly firmly but not so as to distort the stitches, as you join.

Position the **Hind Leg Thigh** cast-on edge to the rump and whip stitch carefully and neatly onto the body. Then whip stitch the **Back of Hind Leg** cast-on edge to the belly.

Note: The leg seam faces towards the tail end.

With yarn **F** work a couple of straight stitches at the front of each hoof, at the top of the seam for the hoof detail.

EARS - MAKE 2 ALIKE

With yarn **CDG** and 3.5mm needles cast on 21 sts for the base of the ear.

Row 1 (WS): Purl

Row 2: Kfb, knit to last st, kfb - 23sts

Rows 3-5: Work 3 rows stocking stitch starting with a purl row

Row 6: Kfb, knit to last st, kfb - 25sts

Rows 7-9: Work 3 rows stocking stitch starting with a purl row

Row 10: K10, skpo, k1, k2tog, knit to end - 23sts

Rows 11, 13, 15, 17, 19, 21, 23, 25, 27: Purl

Row 12: K9, skpo, k1, k2tog, knit to **end - 21sts**

Row 14: K8, skpo, k1, k2tog, knit to **end - 19sts**

Row 16: K7, skpo, k1, k2tog, knit to **end - 17sts**

Row 18: K6, skpo, k1, k2tog, knit to **end - 15sts**

Row 20: K5, skpo, k1, k2tog, knit to **end - 13sts**

Row 22: K4, skpo, k1, k2tog, knit to **end - 11sts**

Row 24: K3, skpo, k1, k2tog, knit to end - 9sts

Row 26: K2, skpo, k1, k2tog, knit to end - 7sts

Row 28: [K2tog] 3 times, k1 - 4sts
Cast off purlwise.

Inner Ear First Side

With yarn **FHI** and 3.5mm needles, with RS facing you, pick up and knit 12 sts between the cast-on edge and the point at the top of the ear (the cast-off).

Row 1 (WS): Purl
Work short rows to shape the inner ear first side:

Short row 1: K11, W+T

Short row 2: P11

Short row 3: K10, W+T

Short row 4: P10

Cut **FHI** and join on yarn **ADG**.

Short row 5: K9, W+T

Short row 6: P9

Short row 7: K8, W+T

Short row 8: P8

Short row 9: K7, W+T

Short row 10: P7

Cast off all sts.

Inner Ear Second Side

With yarn **FHI** and 3.5mm needles, with RS facing you, pick up and knit 12 sts between the point at the top of the ear (the cast-off) and the cast-on edge.

Row 1 (WS): Purl

Row 2: Knit

Work short rows to shape the inner ear second side:

Short row 1: P11, W+T

Short row 2: K11

Short row 3: P10, W+T

Cut **FHI** and join on yarn **ADG**.

Short row 4: K10

Short row 5: P9, W+T

Short row 6: K9

Short row 7: P8, W+T

Short row 8: K8

Short row 9: P7, W+T

Short row 10: K7

Cast off all sts purlwise.

Working on one ear at a time

With RS together, fold the ear so that the cast-off edges meet, and back stitch along the cast-off edges around the ear peak *(see fig. 11, dotted lines)*. Turn out to RS and push the seam into the ear.

Tuck in your yarn ends for stuffing (there's no need to add anything more).

Working on one side of the head at a time place the base of the ear onto the head, referring to photographs for placement, whip stitch neatly to securely join ear to head.

FINISHING DETAILS

The following few extra finishing details are important to get the right look for your fawn so take time over them.

Face shaping

To make the face squish up a little, fold a length of yarn in half and pass the cut ends through a yarn sewing needle. Pass the threaded needle through one side of the head, just under the eye socket, and out the other side of the head, under eye socket. Then pass the needle back through the head to emerge back out where you started and through the loop of the folded yarn. Pull up to squish the face and secure the thread.

Ear shaping

With a new length of yarn, pass the threaded needle through one side of the head, just beneath the outer ear, and out the other side of the head, beneath the ear. Then pass the needle back through the head to emerge back out where you started and through the loop of the folded yarn. Pull up to squish the face at the ears and secure the thread.

White markings

With yarn **F** work a stitch over a knitted stitch to replicate it *(see fig. 12)*, this is called duplicate stitch. Continue to work duplicate stitch to create shapes over the back. You could use pictures of real deer as inspiration or just make it up.

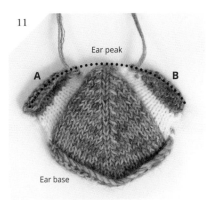

Red Fox

{Vulpes vulpes}

Trickster, sly, mischievous, outwitting and
cunning - all attributed to Mr. (and Mrs!) Fox
- but this benevolent red head symbolises the
victory of intelligence over both malevolence
and brute strength. It's been noted that the fox
will not ever use physical attack, only mental.

You'll never out-fox a fox!

FINISHED SIZE

Approx. 33cm (13in) tall, and 40cm (15¾in) long

YARN

You will need no more than one ball each of:

A: Drops Alpaca in shade 0501 light grey mix

B: Drops Kid Silk in shade 01 off white

C: Drops Flora in shade 02 white

D: Drops Brushed Alpaca Silk in shade 19 curry

E: Drops Alpaca in shade 2915 orange

F: James C Brett Faux Fur Chunky in shade H7 white

G: James C Brett Faux Fur Chunky in shade H4 caramel/white

H: Drops Kid Silk in shade 15 dark brown

I: Drops Flora in shade 06 black

J: Drops Brushed Alpaca Silk in shade 04 light beige

Unless otherwise stated, multiple strands of yarn are used together throughout this pattern. The exact combinations of yarn to be used are indicated by multiple letters (see How to Use This Book).

NEEDLES

3.5mm and 5mm knitting needles

TENSION

17 rows and 11.5 stitches over 5cm (2in) with 3.5mm knitting needles

14 rows and 9.5 stitches over 5cm (2in) with 5mm knitting needles

OTHER TOOLS AND MATERIALS

· 3 large safety pins or stitch holders

· 36 locking stitch markers

· 14mm light brown or amber toy safety eyes

· Toy filling or yarn/fabric scraps

BEGINNING AT THE MUZZLE

With yarn **ABC** and 3.5mm needles, cast on 12 sts.
PM at each end of last row for **Muzzle Marker**.
Row 1 (RS): Kfb, knit to last st, kfb - 14sts
Rows 2-4: Work 3 rows stocking stitch starting with a purl row
Row 5: Kfb, knit to last st, kfb - 16sts
Row 6: P2tog, purl to last 2 sts, p2tog -14sts
Row 7: Cast off 5 sts, knit to last 5 sts, cast off last 5 sts and cut yarn - 4sts

BRIDGE OF THE NOSE

With WS facing you, with yarn **DE** and 3.5mm needles, return to the remaining 4 sts.
Row 1 (WS): Purl
Row 2: Kfb, knit to last st, kfb - 6sts
Rows 3-4: Repeat last 2 rows once - 8sts
Rows 5-9: Work 5 rows stocking stitch starting with a purl row
PM at each end of last row for **Nose Marker**.
Row 10: K2tog, knit to last 2 sts, k2tog - 6sts
Row 11: Purl
Rows 12-13: Repeat last 2 rows once - 4sts
Rows 14-15: Work 2 rows stocking stitch
PM at each end of last row for **Bridge Marker**.
Cast off all 4 bridge sts.

FOREHEAD

With RS facing you, with yarn **DE**, pick up and knit 5 sts across bridge cast-off sts (see General Techniques).
Row 1: Purl
Row 2: Kfb, knit to last st, kfb - 7sts
Row 3: Purl
Row 4-7: Repeat last 2 rows twice - 11sts
Row 8: Kfb, k1, kfb, knit to last 3 sts, kfb, k1, kfb - 15sts
Row 9: Purl
Row 10: Kfb, knit to last st, kfb - 17sts
Row 11: Purl
PM at each end of last row for **Eye Edge Marker**.
Work short rows (see General Techniques) to shape the forehead:
Short row 1: K16, W+T
Short row 2: P15, W+T
Short row 3: K14, W+T
Short row 4: P13, W+T
Short row 5: K12, W+T
Short row 6: P11, W+T
Short row 7: K10, W+T
Short row 8: P9, W+T
Short row 9: K8, W+T
Short row 10: P7, W+T
Short row 11: Knit to end
Cast off forehead sts purlwise.

FOX'S LEFT CHEEK

With RS facing you, return to fox's left nose and muzzle (on your right).

With yarn **BBC** and 3.5mm needles, pick up and knit 12 sts from fox's left **Muzzle Marker** to fox's left **Nose Marker**.

Row 1 (WS): Purl

Row 2: K3, k2tog, k1, k2tog, knit to end - 10sts

Row 3: Purl

Rows 4-5: Repeat last 2 rows once - 8sts

Row 6: Knit to last st, kfb - 9sts

Work short rows to create the fox's left cheek:

Short row 1: P8, W+T

Short row 2: K8

Short row 3: P7, W+T

Short row 4: K7

Short row 5: P6, W+T

Short row 6: K6

Short row 7: P5, W+T

Short row 8: K5

Row 7: Purl

PM at end of last row for **Jaw Marker**.

Cut **BBC** and join **DE** work with yarn **DE**.

Row 8: K9, pick up and knit 10 sts along to fox's left **Nose Marker** - 19sts

Row 9: Purl

Row 10: K2tog, knit to end - 18sts

Rows 11-14: Repeat last 2 rows twice - 16sts

PM at end of last row for **Eye Corner Marker**.

Row 15: Cast off 4 sts purlwise, purl to end - 12sts

PM at end of last row for **Lower Jaw Marker**.

Row 16: K2tog, knit to last 2 sts, k2tog - 10sts

Row 17: Purl

Row 18: K2tog, knit to end - 9sts

PM at end of last row for **Eye Marker**.

Work short rows to create the top of the fox's temple:

Short row 1: P7, W+T

Short row 2: K7

Short row 3: P6, W+T

Short row 4: K6

Row 19: Purl

Cut yarn and leave the 9 left temple stitches on a safety pin.

Add Colour to the Fox's Left Eyebrow

With RS facing you, return to fox's left eye (on your right).

With yarn **DB** and 3.5mm needles pick up and knit 9 sts from fox's left **Bridge Marker** to fox's left **Eye Edge Marker**.

Row 1 (WS): P2tog, purl to end - 8sts

Row 2: K2tog, knit to end - 7sts

Cast off purlwise.

FOX'S RIGHT CHEEK

With RS facing you, return to fox's right nose and muzzle (on your left).

With yarn **BBC** and 3.5mm needles, pick up and knit 12 sts from fox's right **Nose Marker** to fox's right **Muzzle Marker**.

Row 1 (WS): Purl

Row 2: K4, k2tog, k1, k2tog, knit to end - 10sts

Row 3: Purl

Row 4: K2, k2tog, k1, k2tog, knit to end - 8sts

Row 5: Purl

Row 6: Kfb, knit to end - 9sts

Row 7: Purl

Work short rows to create the fox's right cheek:

Short row 1: K8, W+T

Short row 2: P8

Short row 3: K7, W+T

Short row 4: P7

Short row 5: K6, W+T

Short row 6: P6

Short row 7: K5, W+T

Short row 8: P5.

Row 8: Knit.

PM at end of last row for **Jaw Marker**.

Cut **BBC** and join **DE** work with yarn **DE**.

Row 9: P9, pick up and purl 10 sts along to fox's right **Nose Marker** - 19sts

Row 10: Knit to last 2 sts, k2tog - 18sts

Row 11: Purl

Rows 12-15: Repeat last 2 rows twice - 16sts

PM at end of last row for **Eye Corner Marker**.

Row 16: Cast off 4 sts, knit to end - 12sts

PM at end of last row for **Lower Jaw Marker**.

Row 17: P2tog, purl to last 2 sts, p2tog - 10sts

Row 18: Knit

Row 19: P2tog, purl to end - 9sts

PM at end of last row for **Eye Marker**.

Work short rows to create the top of the fox's temple:

Short row 1: K7, W+T

Short row 2: P7

Short row 3: K6, W+T

Short row 4: P6

Cut yarn and leave the 9 right temple stitches on a safety pin.

Add Colour to the Fox's Right Eyebrow

With RS facing you, return to fox's right eye (on your left).

With yarn **DB** and 3.5mm needles pick up and knit 9 sts from fox's right **Eye Edge Marker** to fox's right **Bridge Marker**.

Row 1 (WS): Purl to end p2tog - 8sts

Row 2: K to last 2 sts, k2tog - 7sts

Cast off purlwise.

HEAD AND BACK

With yarn **DE** and 3.5mm needles, slip the 9 left temple stitches from the safety pin onto LH needle with RS facing you, k9, pick up and knit 10 sts across cast-off edge at forehead, slip the 9 right temple stitches from the safety pin onto LH needle with RS facing you, k9 - 28sts.

Row 1 (WS): Purl

PM at each end of last row for **Neck Marker**.

Row 2: K1, kfb, k2, kfb, knit to last 5 sts, kfb, k2, kfb, k1 - 32sts

Row 3: Purl

Join **B** to work with yarn **BDE**.

Row 4: K1, kfb, k4, PM for left **Ear Marker**, k20, PM for right **Ear Marker**, knit to last 2 sts, kfb, k1 - 34sts

Row 5: Purl

Row 6: K12, skpo, PM for left **Inner Ear Marker**, k6, PM for right **Inner Ear Marker**, k2tog, knit to end - 32sts

Row 7: Purl

Row 8: K11, skpo, k6, k2tog, knit to end - 30sts

Row 9: Purl

Row 10: K11, PM for left **Ear Back Marker**, k8, PM for right **Ear Back Marker**, knit to end

Row 11: Purl

Cut **BDE**, change to 5mm needles and join yarn **G**.

Row 12: Knit

PM at each end of last row for **Neck Fur Markers**.

Row 13: Purl

Row 14: K11, skpo, k4, k2tog, knit to end - 28sts

Row 15: Purl

Row 16: Kfb, k9, skpo, k4, k2tog, k to last st, kfb

Row 17: Purl

Rows 18-23: Repeat last 2 rows three times

Rows 24-25: Work 2 rows stocking stitch

Cut **G** and join yarn **BDEH**.

Row 26: Cast on 6 sts, PM for left **Front Marker**, knit to end - 34sts

Row 27: Cast on 6 sts, PM for right **Front Marker**, purl to end - 40sts

Row 28: K16, skpo, k4, k2tog, knit to end - 38sts

Row 29: Purl

Row 30: K15, skpo, k4, k2tog, knit to end - 36sts

Row 31: Purl

Row 32: K15, skpo, k2, k2tog, knit to end - 34sts

Row 33: Purl

Row 34: K2tog, k12, skpo, k2, k2tog, knit to last 2 sts, k2tog - 30sts

Row 35: Purl

Row 36: K2tog, k10, skpo, k2, k2tog, knit to last 2 sts, k2tog - 26sts

Row 37: Purl

Row 38: K2tog, k8, skpo, k2, k2tog, knit to last 2 sts, k2tog - 22sts

Row 39: Purl

Row 40: Cast off 5 sts for left **Side Seam**, knit to end - 17sts

Row 41: Cast off 5 sts for right **Side Seam**, purl to end - 12sts

Row 42: Cast on 6 sts for left **Side Seam**, knit to end - 18sts

Row 43: Cast on 6 sts for right **Side Seam**, purl to end - 24sts

Rows 44-53: Work 10 rows stocking stitch

HIND LEGS - UPPER PART

Cut **EH** and join **J** to work with yarn **BDJ**.

Row 54: Cast on 10 sts for fox's left hind leg, PM for left **Upper Thigh Marker,** knit to end - 34sts

Row 55: Cast on 10 sts for fox's right hind leg, PM for right **Upper Thigh Marker,** purl to end - 44sts

Work short rows to create the top of the left leg:

Short row 1: K11, W+T

Short row 2: P1, W+T

Short row 3: K2, W+T

Short row 4: P3, W+T

Short row 5: K4, W+T

Short rows 6-17: Continue as set, working longer rows each time until…

Short row 18: P17, p2tog - 43sts

Short row 19: Knit to end

Work short rows to create the top of the right leg:

Short row 1: P11, W+T

Short row 2: K1, W+T

Short row 3: P2, W+T

Short row 4: K3, W+T

Short row 5: P4, W+T

Short rows 6-17: Continue as set, working longer rows each time until…

Short row 18: K17, k2tog - 42sts

Short row 19: Purl to end

Row 56: K2tog, knit to last 2 sts, k2tog - 40sts

Row 57: Purl

Rows 58-63: Repeat last 2 rows three times - 34sts

Row 64: K2tog, k12, skpo, k2, k2tog, knit to last 2 sts, k2tog - 30sts

Row 65: Purl

Row 66: K2tog, k10, skpo, k2, k2tog, knit to last 2 sts, k2tog - 26sts

Row 67: Purl

Row 68: K2tog, k8, skpo, k3, k2tog, knit to last 2 sts, k2tog - 22sts

Row 69: Purl

Row 70: K2tog, k6, skpo, k3, k2tog, knit to last 2 sts, k2tog - 18sts

Row 71: Purl

Row 72: K2tog, k4, skpo, k3, k2tog, knit to last 2 sts, k2tog - 14sts

Rows 73-78: Work 6 rows stocking stitch starting with a purl row

PM at each end of last row for **Tail Markers.**

BRUSH

Cut BDJ and join yarn G.

Rows 1-20: Work 20 rows stocking stitch

Cut G and join yarn F.

Row 21: K2tog, knit to last 2 sts, **k2tog - 12sts**

Row 22: Purl

Rows 23-30: Repeat last 2 rows four **times - 4sts**

PM at each end of last row for **Tail Fold Markers.**

Row 31: Kfb, knit to last st, kfb - 6sts

Row 32: Purl

Rows 33-44: Repeat last 2 rows six **times - 14sts**

Cut F and join yarn G.

Rows 45-54: Work 10 rows **stocking stitch**

Row 55: K2tog, knit to last 2 sts, **k2tog - 12sts**

Rows 56-62: Work 7 rows stocking stitch

Row 63: K2tog, knit to last 2 sts, k2tog - 10sts

Cast off.

CHIN AND THROAT

Return to the cast-on edge at the muzzle from the beginning of the pattern.

With RS facing you, with yarn **BBC** and 3.5mm needles, pick up and knit 8 sts across the cast-on edge from fox's right **Muzzle Marker** to fox's left **Muzzle Marker** (*see fig. 1, A to B*).

Remove **Muzzle Markers**.

Work short rows to create fox's chin:

Short row 1: P5, W+T

Short row 2: K2, W+T

Short row 3: P3, W+T

Short row 4: K4, W+T

Short row 5: P5, W+T

Short row 6: K6, W+T

Short row 7: Purl to end

Rows 1-8: Work 8 rows stocking stitch

PM at each end of last row for **Throat Markers.**

Rows 9-12: Work 4 rows stocking stitch

Row 13: Kfb, knit to last st, kfb - 10sts

Row 14: Purl

Rows 15-16: Repeat last 2 rows once - 12sts

PM at each end of last row for **Lower Throat Markers.**

Stop knitting and slip the 12 neck sts onto a stitch holder whilst you sew the face seams.

Sewing Nose and Forehead Seams

Working on one side of the face at a time, match the **Eye Corner Marker** with **Bridge Marker** and mattress stitch to join along the side of the bridge of the nose from **Eye Corner Marker** along to the **Nose Marker**.

Remove **Eye Corner**, **Nose**, and **Bridge Marker**.

Work a couple of small stitches to join and tidy just the corner of the eye lid colour detail.

Working on one side of the forehead at a time, match the **Eye Edge Marker** with the **Eye Marker** and ease the seam together. Mattress stitch from the **Eye Marker** to the temple.

Remove **Eye** and **Eye Edge Markers**.

Sewing Chin and Throat Seam

Working on one side at a time, match the **Jaw Marker** to the **Throat Marker** and mattress stitch from the muzzle to the **Jaw Marker**. Then match the **Lower Jaw Marker** to the **Lower Throat Marker** and mattress stitch from the **Jaw Marker** to the **Lower Jaw Marker** (*see fig. 2*).

Remove **Jaw**, **Lower Jaw**, **Throat**, and **Lower Throat Markers**.

THROAT

With yarn **BBC** and 3.5mm needle, slip the 12 neck stitches from the holder onto LH needle with RS facing you.

Row 17: K12, pick up and knit 7 sts up to fox's left **Neck Marker** - 19sts

Row 18: Purl, pick up and purl 7 sts up to fox's right **Neck Marker** - 26sts

Rows 19-20: Work 2 rows stocking stitch

Cut **BBC** and join yarn **F**.

Row 21: Knit

Row 22: P2tog, purl to last 2 sts, p2tog - 24sts

Rows 23-26: Repeat last 2 rows twice - 20sts

PM at each end of last row for **Fur Markers**.

Rows 27-46: Work 20 rows stocking stitch

PM at each end of last row for **Breast Markers**.

Cut **F**, change to 5mm needles and join yarn **BCJ**.

Rows 47-52: Work 6 rows stocking stitch

Row 53: K6, skpo, k4, k2tog, knit to end - 18sts

Row 54: Purl

Row 55: K6, skpo, k2, k2tog, knit to end - 16sts

Row 56: Purl

Row 57: K6, skpo, k2tog, knit to end - 14sts

Row 58: Purl

PM at each end of last row for **Belly Markers**.

Rows 59-68: Work 10 rows stocking stitch

Row 69: K2tog, knit to last 2sts, k2tog - 12sts

Row 70: Purl

Rows 71-78: Repeat last 2 rows 4 times - 4sts

Rows 79-84: Work 6 rows stocking stitch

PM at each end of last row for **Inner Thigh Markers**.

Cast off for tail end.

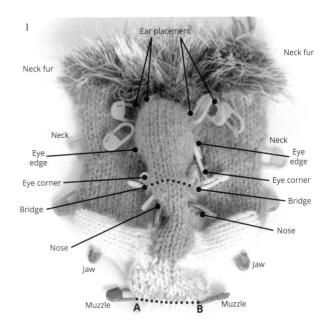

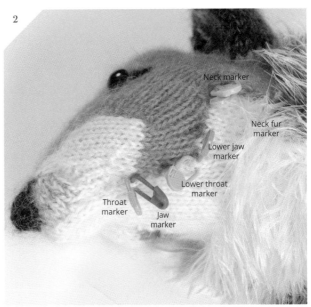

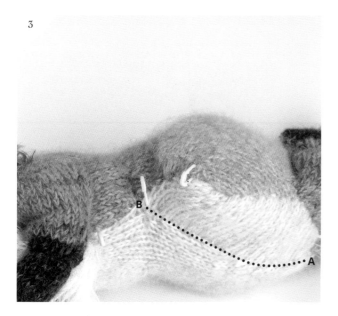

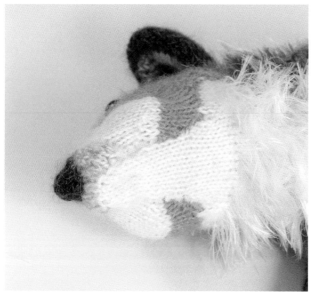

FOX'S LEFT INNER THIGH

With RS facing you, with yarn **BCJ** and 5mm needles, pick up and knit 26 sts across row ends from fox's left **Inner Thigh Marker** to fox's left **Belly Marker** (*see fig. 3, dotted line from A to B*).

Rows 1-5: Work 5 rows stocking stitch starting with a purl row
PM at end of last row for **Inner Tail Marker**.

Row 6: K2tog, knit to last st, kfb

Row 7: Purl

Rows 8-11: Repeat last 2 rows twice

Row 12: [K2tog] twice, k18, [k2tog] twice - 22sts
PM at end of last row for **Inner Upper Thigh Marker**.

Cast off all front of inner thigh sts purlwise.

FOX'S RIGHT INNER THIGH

With RS facing you, with yarn **BCJ** and 5mm needles, pick up and knit 26 sts across row ends from fox's right **Belly Marker** to fox's right **Inner Thigh Marker**.

Rows 1-4: Work 4 rows stocking stitch starting with a purl row
PM at end of last row for **Inner Tail Marker**.

Row 5: Purl

Row 6: Kfb, knit to last 2 sts, k2tog

Row 7: Purl

Rows 8-11: Repeat last 2 rows twice

Row 12: [K2tog] twice, k18, [k2tog] twice - 22sts
PM at start of last row for **Inner Upper Thigh Marker**.

Cast off all front of inner thigh sts purlwise.

Remove **Inner Thigh Markers**.

NECK AND BODY SEAMS

Join Side Seams

Working on one side of the body at a time, with RS together, match the **Side Seam** cast-off edge with the **Side Seam** cast-on edge and back stitch to join. Turn out to RS.

Join Inner to Outer Thigh

Note: You may find it easier if you pin each of these seams before sewing.

Working on one side at a time, with RS together match the end of the **Side Seam** with the **Belly Marker,** then match the **Upper Thigh Marker** with the **Inner Upper Thigh Marker**. Ease together and back stitch from the **Side Seam** to the **Upper Thigh Marker**.

Remove **Belly Markers**, **Upper Thigh Markers** and **Inner Upper Thigh Markers**.

Now match the **Tail Marker** with the **Inner Tail Marker** and ease together, then back stitch from the end of the previous seam to the **Tail Marker**. Turn out to RS.

Remove **Inner Tail Markers**.

Join Neck and Jaw

Working on one side at a time, match **Neck Fur Maker** with the **Fur Marker** and ease together. Mattress stitch from the **Neck Marker** to the **Neck Fur Maker**.

Remove **Neck** and **Fur Markers**.

Join Front to Breast

Working on one side at a time, match the **Front Marker** with the **Breast Marker** and ease together. Mattress stitch from the **Neck Fur Marker** to the **Front Maker**.

Remove **Neck Fur** and **Breast Markers**.

Stuff the Head

Tuck in yarn ends and stuff the head, but not too much. The shaping around the muzzle and at the sides of the nose are meant to be quite soft, not firm and bulging.

Join Front to Belly

Working on one side at a time, mattress stitch from the **Side Seam** to the **Front Marker**.

Remove **Front Markers**.

Stuff the Body

Tuck in yarn ends and stuff the body through the opening at the tail end, making sure the stuffing fills out the upper thigh shaping nicely, but not over stuffing.

Tail Seams

Fold tail at the **Tail Fold Markers** with WS together. Match the cast-off edge of the tail to the stitches between the two **Tail Markers**, then whip stitch to join along the tail sides. The tail is not stuffed.

Remove **Tail Fold** and **Tail Markers**.

EYES (MAKE TWO ALIKE)

With yarn **II** and 3.5mm needles, cast on 7 sts.

Rows 1-6: Work 6 rows stocking stitch Cast off.

Sewing the Eyes

With RS together, fold each eye in half at the row ends, cast-on edge to cast-off edge.

Working on one side at a time whip stitch along the row ends. Turn out to RS and open out into an almond-like shape with the seamed ends tucked underneath.

Attach the toy eye in the centre of the knitted eye then insert the knitted eye into the left eye socket *(see fig. 4)*. Using yarn **H** carefully whip stitch around the eye to join it into the eye socket.

NOSE

With yarn **HI** and 3.5mm needles, cast on 8 sts.

Rows 1-2: Work 2 rows stocking stitch
Row 3: K2tog, knit to last 2 sts, k2tog - 6sts
Row 4: Purl
Row 5: K2, k2tog, k2 - 5sts
Row 6: Purl.
PM at each end of last row for **Nose Fold Markers**.
Row 7: Cast on 3 sts, knit to end - 8sts
Row 8: Cast on 3 sts, purl to end - 11sts
Rows 9-10: Work 2 rows stocking stitch Cast off.

Sewing on the Nose

Working on one side at a time, with RS together, fold nose at the **Nose Fold Markers**, matching row end of initial cast-on with row end of cast-off. Back stitch to join row ends between initial cast-on and **Nose Fold Marker**, to cast-on edge (from Rows 7 or 8) and row ends before cast-off. Turn out to RS, and stuff the nose a little with yarn **I**.

Remove **Nose Fold Markers**.

Fit the nose over the beige muzzle and whip stitch in place *(see fig. 5)*. The cast-on edge from beginning of nose becomes the top of the nose, the cast-off edge lies at the mouth seam.

4

5

EARS (MAKE TWO ALIKE)

Outer Ear

With yarn **DE** and 3.5mm needles, cast on 21 sts.

Row 1 (WS): Purl
Row 2: Kfb, knit to last st, kfb - 23sts
Row 3 (WS): Purl
Cut **DE** and join yarn **IIH**.
Rows 4-9: Work 6 rows stocking stitch
Row 10: K9, skpo, k1, k2tog, knit to end - 21sts
Row 11: Purl
Row 12: K8, skpo, k1, k2tog, knit to end - 19sts
Row 13: Purl
Row 14: K7, skpo, k1, k2tog, knit to end - 17sts
Row 15: P3, p2tog, p7, p2tog, purl to end - 15sts
Row 16: K5, skpo, k1, k2tog, knit to end - 13sts
Row 17: [P3, p2tog] twice, purl to end - 11sts
Row 18: K3, skpo, k1, k2tog, knit to end - 9sts
Row 19: P3, p3tog, purl to end - 7sts
Row 20: K2tog, k3, k2tog - 5sts
Row 21: P1, p3tog, p1 - 3sts
Row 22: K3tog
Fasten off at ear peak.

Inner Ear

With RS facing you, with yarn **IIH** and 3.5mm needles, and beginning at the base of the ear, pick up and knit 20 sts (10 sts either side of the ear peak) all around the outer edge of the outer ear, working from ear base on side one to ear peak to ear base on side two.

Row 1 (WS): Purl
Cut **IIH** and join yarn **BCJ**.
Work short rows to shape the inner ear side one:
Short row 1: K9, W+T
Short row 2: P9
Short row 3: K8, W+T
Short row 4: P8
Short row 5: K7, W+T
Short row 6: P7
Cast off 10 sts, knit to end.
Work short rows to shape the inner ear side two:
Short row 1: P9, W+T
Short row 2: K9
Short row 3: P8, W+T
Short row 4: K8
Short row 5: P7, W+T
Short row 6: K7
Cast off 10 sts purlwise.

With WS together, flatten the inner ear down to lay inside the outer ear and carefully whip stitch around the cast-off edges and along the row ends of the inner ear so joining to the outer ear.

Attach Ears to Head

Working on one ear at a time place the base of the ear onto the head so that the front corners of the ear 'triangle' match with the **Ear Marker** and **Inner Ear Markers**, and the centre of the ear base matches with the **Ear Back Marker** (*see fig. 6*), then whip stitch neatly and securely to join ear to head.

When you've joined the ear back, pull the ear inner onto the head and whip stitch that in place too.

Remove **Ear**, **Inner Ear**, and **Ear Back Markers**.

FOX'S LEFT FORELEG

With yarn **DEH** and 5mm needles, cast on 10 sts for top of left foreleg shoulder.

Row 1 (RS): Kfb, knit to last st, kfb - 12sts
Row 2: Purl
Rows 3-4: Repeat last 2 rows once - 14sts
Rows 5-8: Work 4 rows stocking stitch
Row 9 (RS): K2tog, knit to last 2 sts, k2tog - 12sts
Row 10: Purl
Rows 11-12: Repeat last 2 rows once - 10sts
Row 13: Cast on 10 sts for back of left foreleg, knit to end - 20sts
Cut **E** and join **I** to work with yarn **DHI**.
Rows 14-16: Work 3 rows stocking stitch
Cut **D** and join **I** to work with yarn **HII**.
Rows 17-36: Work 20 rows stocking stitch

Fox's Left Front Paw

Row 37: K8, kfb, k2, kfb, knit to end - 22sts
Row 38: Purl
Row 39: K9, kfb, k2, kfb, knit to end - 24sts
Row 40: Purl
Row 41: K10, kfb, k2, kfb, knit to end - 26sts
Row 42: Purl
Work short rows for fox's front paw:
Short row 1: K21, W+T

Short row 2: P16, W+T
Short row 3: K15, W+T
Short row 4: P14, W+T
Short row 5: K13, W+T
Short row 6: P12, W+T
Short row 7: K11, W+T
Short row 8: P10, W+T
Short row 9: K9, W+T
Short row 10: P8, W+T
Short row 11: Knit to end
Cast off purlwise.

FOX'S RIGHT FORELEG

With yarn **DEH** and 5mm needles, cast on 10sts for top of right foreleg shoulder.

Rows 1-12: Work as for **Fox's Left Foreleg Rows 1-12**

Row 13: Knit

Row 14: Cast on 10 sts for back of right foreleg, purl to end - 20sts

Cut **E** and join **I** to work with yarn **DHI**.

Rows 15-17: Work 3 rows stocking stitch

Cut **D** and join **I** to work with yarn **HII**.

Rows 18-36: Work 19 rows stocking stitch

Fox's Right Front Paw

Work as for **Fox's Left Front Paw**.

Working on one foreleg at a time at a time, with WS together fold the cast-off edge in half and mattress stitch to join along the bottom of the paw.

Mattress stitch to join the row ends for the back of the leg, a stuff fairly firmly through the cast-on edge.

Whip stitch around the cast-on edge to join leg part of foreleg to the body over the 'front' cast-on section just beneath the fur at the neck and at the seam that joins the back to breast. Add a little bit of stuffing just to pad out the 'shoulder' a little.

HIND FEET (MAKE TWO ALIKE)

With yarn **DEH** and 5mm needles, cast on 10sts for leg part of the foot.

Rows 1-10: Work 10 rows stocking stitch

Cut **H** and join **I** to work with yarn **DEI**.

Row 11: Cast on 20 sts, knit to end

Rows 12-14: Work 3 rows stocking stitch starting with a purl row

Cut **DE** and join **HI** to work with yarn **HII**.

Work short rows to shape foot pad - side one:

Short row 1: K13, W+T
Short row 2: P13
Short row 3: K12, W+T
Short row 4: P12
Short row 5: K11, W+T
Short row 6: P11
Short row 7: K10, W+T
Short row 8: P10

Rows 15-30: Work 16 rows stocking stitch

Work short rows to shape foot pad - side two:

Short row 1: K13, W+T
Short row 2: P13
Short row 3: K12, W+T
Short row 4: P12
Short row 5: K11, W+T
Short row 6: P11
Short row 7: K10, W+T
Short row 8: P10

Cut **HI** and join **DE** to work with yarn **DEI**.

Rows 31-32: Work 2 rows stocking stitch

Row 33: Cast off 20 sts, knit to end - 10sts

Cut **I** and join **H** to work with yarn **DEH**.

Rows 34-43: Work 10 rows stocking stitch starting with a purl row

Cast off all sts for top of leg part of foot.

With WS together, fold foot in half matching initial cast-on edge to final cast-off edge, and mattress stitch from this edge down to the top of the foot, along the top of the foot, and down the row ends to the fold.

Mattress stitch the remaining row ends for the back of foot.

Stuff fairly firmly through the open edge at the leg part of the foot.

Whip stitch around the open edge to join leg part of foot to the body at thigh.

With yarn **A** work four straight stitches over the feet, pulling each stitch so that it draws the stuffed paw inwards to create a toe-divide.

Mallard Duck

{Anas platyrhynchos}

The duck is a spiritual totem. These birds
are connected with the spiritual world
by many bonds. Because of their various
capabilities, ducks are believed to be able
to travel between the realms of spiritual
forces and the world of our reality.

FINISHED SIZE

Approx. 17cm (6¾in) tall, and 26cm (10¼in) long from bill tip to tail tip

YARN

You will need no more than one ball each of:

A: Drops Lima in shade 5610 brown

B: Drops Lima in shade 0619 beige mix

C: Drops Lima in shade 9015 grey

D: Drops Lima in shade 0100 off white

E: Drops Karisma in shade 07 bright blue

F: Drops Lima in shade 0519 dark grey mix

G: Drops Karisma in shade 47 forest green

H: Drops Lima in shade 0701 petrol mix

I: Drops Karisma in shade 79 lemon punch

J: Drops Lima in shade 2923 goldenrod

Unless otherwise stated, multiple strands of yarn are used together throughout this pattern. The exact combinations of yarn to be used are indicated by multiple letters (see How to Use This Book).

NEEDLES

5mm (a pair and a spare), and 3.75mm knitting needles

TENSION

14 rows and 9.5 stitches over 5cm (2in) with 5mm knitting needles

OTHER TOOLS AND MATERIALS

· 16 locking stitch markers

· 6mm black toy safety eyes

· Toy filling or yarn/fabric scraps

· Black embroidery thread or wool to embroider the beak

BEGINNING AT THE BREAST

With yarn **AB** and 5mm needles cast on 30 sts.

Row 1 (RS): K13, kfb, k2, kfb, knit to end - 32sts

Row 2: Purl

Row 3: K3, kfb, k2, kfb, k18, kfb, k2, kfb, k3 - 36sts

Row 4: Purl

Work short rows (see General Techniques) to shape the Breast Right Side:

Short row 1: K13, W+T

Short row 2: P13

Short row 3: K12, W+T

Short row 4: P12

Short row 5: K11, W+T

Short row 6: P11

Short rows 7-18: Continue as set, making shorter and shorter rows until…

Short row 19: K4, W+T

Short row 20: P4

Row 5 (RS): Knit

Work short rows to shape the Breast Left Side:

Short row 1: P13, W+T

Short row 2: K13

Short row 3: P12, W+T

Short row 4: K12

Short row 5: P11, W+T

Short row 6: K11

Short rows 7-18: Continue as set, making shorter and shorter rows until…

Short row 19: P4, W+T

Short row 20: K4

Row 6 (WS): Purl

Work short rows to shape the Keel Right Side:

Short row 1: K10, W+T

Short row 2: P7, W+T

Short row 3: K6, W+T

Short row 4: P5, W+T

Short row 5: K4, W+T

Short row 6: P3, W+T

Short row 7: Knit to end

Work short rows to shape the Keel Left Side:

Short row 1: P10, W+T

Short row 2: K7, W+T

Short row 3: P6, W+T

Short row 4: K5, W+T

Short row 5: P4, W+T

Short row 6: K3, W+T

Short row 7: Purl to end

BACK

Cut **A** and join **C** to work with yarn **BC**.

Row 7 (RS): K10, skpo, k12, k2tog, knit to end - 34sts

Now separate back feathers from breast to work on just the 14 back sts:

Row 8: P10, PM in last stitch worked for **Keel Marker**, p14 (these are the back sts), turn

Row 9: Skpo, k10, k2tog - 12 back sts

Row 10, 12, 14, 16, 18: Purl

Row 11: Skpo, k8, k2tog - 10 back sts

Row 13: Skpo, k6, k2tog - 8 back sts

Row 15: Skpo, k4, k2tog - 6 back sts

Row 17: Skpo, k2, k2tog - 4 back sts

Row 19: Skpo, k2tog - 2 back sts

Row 20: P2tog

Fasten off.

KEEL

Using your spare needle, rearrange the remaining two sets of 10 sts so that the previous start and end of row are next to each other on the needle, the **Keel Marker** is in the first stitch of the next row, and you are ready to work a RS row.

Remove the **Keel Marker**.

Rejoin yarn **BD** and work across all 20 sts to join the two sections:

Row 1 (RS): K2, kfb, k4, kfb, k4, kfb, k4, kfb, k2 - 24sts

Row 2: Purl pulling tight as you work across the join

Row 3: K3, kfb, k5, kfb, k4, kfb, k5, kfb, k3 - 28sts

Row 4: Purl

Row 5: K4, kfb, k6, kfb, k4, kfb, k6, kfb, k4 - 32sts

Row 6: Purl

Row 7: K5, kfb, k7, kfb, k4, kfb, k7, kfb, k5 - 36sts

Row 8: Purl

Cut **B** and join on **C** to work with yarn **CD**.

Rows 9-16: Work 8 rows stocking stitch

Row 17: K4, skpo, k4, k2tog, k12, skpo, k4, k2tog, knit to end - 32sts

Row 18: Purl

Row 19: K3, skpo, k4, k2tog, k10, skpo, k4, k2tog, knit to end - 28sts

Rows 20-32: Work 13 rows stocking stitch starting with a purl row

PM at each end of the last row for **Tail to Keel Marker**

Cut **C** and join **D** to work with yarn **DD**.

Row 33 (RS): K2, skpo, k4, k2tog, k8, skpo, k4, k2tog, knit to end - 24sts

Rows 34-36: Work 3 rows stocking stitch

Row 37: K1, skpo, k4, k2tog, k6, skpo, k4, k2tog, k1 - 20sts

Row 38: Purl

Row 39: Skpo, k4, k2tog, k4, skpo, k4, k2tog - 16sts

Row 40: Purl

Row 41: Skpo, k2, k2tog, k4, skpo, k2, k2tog - 12sts

Row 42: Purl

TAIL

Cut **DD** and join yarn **FF** to work the Tail.

Row 43 (RS): Skpo, knit to last 2 sts, k2tog - 10sts

Row 44: Purl

Rows 45-48 dec): Rep last 2 rows twice - 6sts

PM at each end of last row for **Tail Fold Marker**.

Row 49: Kfb, k to last 2 sts, kfb - 8sts

Row 50: Purl

Rows 51-52: Repeat last 2 rows once - 10sts

Note: Two 'picots' are worked on the next row to create the pair of curled tail feathers.

Row 53 (RS): Kfb, k1, cast on 6 sts then cast off those 6 sts (first picot worked), k4, cast on 6 sts then cast off those 6 sts (second picot worked), k1, kfb - 12sts

Rows 54-56: Work 3 rows stocking stitch starting with a purl row

Row 57: K6, PM in gap before next stitch for **Tail Marker**, k6

Rows 58-60: Work 3 rows stocking stitch starting with a purl row
Cast off.

PM each end of cast-off edge for **Tail to Keel Marker**.

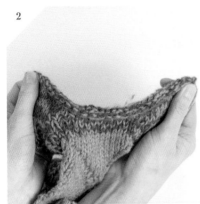

LEFT WING

With RS facing you, with yarn **BC** and 5mm needles, pick up and knit 11 sts (see General Techniques) along the left side of the back from where the back divides from the breast to the fastened off tip (see fig. 1).

Row 1 (WS): Pfb, purl to end - 12sts
Row 2: Kfb, knit to end - 13sts
Row 3: Cast on 12sts, purl all 25 sts
Row 4: Skpo, knit to last 2 sts, kfb, k1
Row 5: Purl
Rows 6-11: Repeat last 2 rows three times
Row 12: Skpo, knit to last 2 sts, k2tog - 23sts

PM on last stitch of last row for **Tail Marker**.

Row 13: Purl

Work short rows to shape the curl of the left wing:

Short row 1: K20, W+T
Short row 2: P17, W+T
Short row 3: K16, W+T
Short row 4: P15, W+T
Short row 5: K14, W+T
Short row 6: P13, W+T
Short row 7: K12, W+T
Short row 8: P11, W+T
Short row 9: K15 sts to last 2 sts, k2tog - 22sts
Row 14 (WS): Purl

Cut **C** and join on **A** to work with yarn **AB**.

Row 15 (RS): Skpo, knit to last 2 sts, k2tog - 20sts
Row 16: P2tog, purl to end - 19sts

The next few rows are worked in intarsia to add stripes. Prepare a 75cm (30in) length of each of yarns **C**, **D** and **E** ready to join on. Use a single strand of each of these colours.

Row 17: Skpo, k5 in **AB**; k2 in **D**, k6 in **E**; k2, k2tog in **C** - 17sts
Row 18: P4 in **C**; p6 in **E**; p2 in **D**; purl to end in **AB**
Row 19: Skpo, k2 in **AB**; k2 in **D**, k6 in **E**; k3, k2tog in **C** - 15sts
Row 20: P5 in **C**; p6 in **E**; p2 in **D**; purl to end in **AB**

Cast off in colours as set.

RIGHT WING

With RS facing you, with yarn **BC** and 5mm needles, pick up and knit 11 sts along the right side of the back from the fastened off tip to where the back divides from the breast.

Row 1 (WS): Purl to last st, pfb - 12sts
Row 2: Knit to last st, kfb - 13sts

Row 3: Purl
Row 4: Cast on 12sts, knit all 25 sts
Row 5: P2tog, purl to end - 24sts
Row 6: K1, kfb, knit to end - 25sts
Rows 7-12: Repeat last 2 rows three times
Row 13: Purl

PM on last stitch of last row for **Tail Marker**.

Row 14: Skpo, knit to last 2 sts, k2tog - 23sts

Work short rows to shape the curl of the right wing:

Short row 1: P20, W+T
Short row 2: K17, W+T
Short row 3: P16, W+T
Short row 4: K15, W+T
Short row 5: P14, W+T
Short row 6: K13, W+T
Short row 7: P12, W+T
Short row 8: K11, W+T
Short row 9: P15 sts to last 2 sts, p2tog - 22sts

Cut **C** and join on **A** to work with yarn **AB**.

Row 15 (RS): Skpo, knit to last 2 sts, k2tog - 20sts
Row 16: Purl to last 2 sts, p2tog - 19sts

Prepare a 75cm (30in) length of each of yarns **C**, **D** and **E** for the intarsia on the following rows.

Row 17: Skpo, k2 in **C**; k6 in **E**; k2 in **D**; k5, k2tog in **AB** - 17sts
Row 18: P5 in **AB**; p2 in **D**; p6 in **E**; p4 in **C**
Row 19: Skpo, k3 in **C**; k6 in **E**; k2 in **D**; k2, k2tog in **AB** - 15sts
Row 20: P2 in **AB**; p2 in **D**; p6 in **E**; p5 in **C**

Cast off in colours as set.

NECK

Return to the cast-on row at the start. With RS facing you, with yarn **AB** and 5mm needles, pick up and knit 28 sts along that cast-on edge (see fig. 2).

Row 1 (WS): P2tog, purl to last 2 sts, p2tog - 26sts
Row 2: K1, skpo, k8, kfb, k2, kfb, knit to last 3 sts, k2tog, k1
Row 3: Purl
Rows 4-5: Repeat last 2 rows once

Cut **AB** and join on yarn **DD** for the white collar.

Work short rows for White Collar Right Side:

Short row 1: K1, skpo, k7, turn - 25sts
Short row 2: P9, turn

Holding **DD** behind the work, join yarn **GH** and continue as follows:

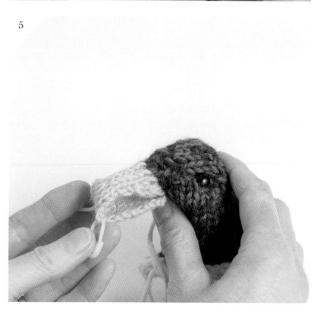

Row 6: K1, skpo, k5, k2tog, k5 in **GH**; k7, k2tog, k1 in **DD** - 22sts
Work short rows for White Collar Left Side:
Short row 1: P9 in **DD**, cut **DD**, turn
Short row 2: Knit to last 3 sts, k2tog, k1 in **GH** - 21sts
Continue with yarn **GH**:
Row 7: P7, p2tog, purl to end - 20sts
Row 8: K1, skpo, k5, kfb, k2, kfb, knit to last 3 sts, k2tog, k1
Row 9: Purl
Row 10: Kfb, k8, k2tog, knit to last st, kfb - 21sts
Row 11: Purl
Row 12: Kfb, k7, skpo, k1, k2tog, knit to last st, kfb
Row 13: Purl

HEAD

Shape Head Right Side with short rows:
Short row 1: K7, W+T
Short row 2: P6, W+T
Short row 3: K5, W+T
Short row 4: P4, W+T
Short row 5: K3, W+T
Short row 6: P2, W+T
Short row 7: Knit to end
Shape Head Left Side with short rows:
Short row 1: P7, W+T
Short row 2: K6, W+T
Short row 3: P5, W+T
Short row 4: K4, W+T
Short row 5: P3, W+T
Short row 6: K2, W+T
Shape back of head with short rows:
Short row 7: P10, W+T
Short row 8: K6, W+T
Short row 9: P5, W+T
Short row 10: K4, W+T
Short row 11: P3, W+T
Short row 12: K2, W+T
Short row 13: P6, turn
Now work the top of the head on the centre 9 sts:
Row 1: K2, kfb, k3, kfb, k2 - 11sts
Row 2: P11
Row 3: K3, kfb, k3, kfb, k3 - 13sts
Row 4: P13
Shape the very front of head:
Row 5: K5, k3tog, k5 - 11sts
Row 6: P2tog, p7, p2tog - 9sts
Row 7: Skpo, k1, k3tog, k1, k2tog - 5sts
Row 8: P1, p3tog, p1 - 3sts
Cast off all 3 front of head sts.
Working on one side at a time rejoin yarn **GH** and cast off the 6 sts, as set, from the sides of the head.
Working on one side at a time and with RS together ease the cast-off edge at the side of the head with the row ends from the top of the head (see fig. 3), and back stitch together.
Position and fit the eyes, referring to photographs for placement and making sure the eyes are level with each other.
Join neck seam with mattress stitch (see fig. 4).

BEAK

With yarn **I** and 3.75mm needles cast on 10 sts.

Row 1: Skpo, knit to last 2 sts, k2tog - 8sts

Row 2: Purl

Row 3: Skpo, knit to last 2 sts, k2tog - 6sts

Rows 4-6: Work 3 rows stocking stitch

Row 7: K2, [kfb] twice, k2 - 8sts

Row 8: Purl

Row 9: K1, skpo, k2, k2tog, k1 - 6sts

Row 10: Purl

Row 11: K1, kfb k2, kfb, k1 - 8sts

Row 12: Purl

PM at each end of last row for **Beak Fold Markers**

Rows 13-14: Work 2 rows stocking stitch

Row 15: K1, skpo, k2, k2tog, k1 - 6sts

Rows 16-18: Work 3 rows stocking stitch starting with a purl row

Row 19: K1, skpo, k2tog, k1 - 4sts

Cast off purlwise.

Carefully press the beak (first checking the yarn manufacturer's guidance about pressing).

Position the cast-on edge under the 'V' at the front of the head *(see fig. 5)* and carefully whip stitch it into place.

Fold the beak at the **Beak Fold Markers**, WS together, and join the cast-off edge to the neck about 1cm (½in) down from where you've joined the top of the beak *(see fig. 6)*.

Carefully whip stitch along each beak side to sandwich the beak together.

Optional: You could add wire to the beak before sewing it closed.

With some black thread or yarn embroider on the black details as shown. It's worth taking time over this to get it looking just right!

Tuck in yarn ends and stuff the head and neck now.

7

Right wing

Left wing

8

9

WEBBED FEET - MAKE 2 ALIKE

With yarns **IJ** and 5mm needles cast on 4 sts.

Rows 1-5: Work 5 rows stocking stitch starting with a knit row

Work top of foot:

Row 6 (RS): Kfb, purl to last st, kfb - 6sts
Row 7 (WS): P1, k2, m1, k2, p1 - 7sts
Row 8: Kfb, p2, k1, p2, kfb - 9sts
Row 9: P1, k3, p1, k3, p1
Row 10: Kfb, p3, k1, p3, kfb - 11sts
Row 11: P1, k4, p1, k4, p1
Row 12: Kfb, p4, k1, p4, kfb - 13sts
Row 13: P1, k5, p1, k5, p1.

PM at each end of last row for **Foot Fold Markers**.

Work bottom of foot:

Row 14 (RS): Skpo, p4, k1, p4, k2tog - 11sts
Row 15: P1, k4, p1, k4, p1
Row 16: Skpo, p3, k1, p3, k2tog - 9sts
Row 17: P1, k3, p1, k3, p1
Row 18: Skpo, p1, k3tog, p1, k2tog - 5sts
Row 19: P1, k1, P1, k1, p1
Row 20: K1, p2tog, p1, k1 - 4sts
Rows 21-26: Work 6 rows stocking stitch

Cast off purlwise.

Fold the foot in half at the **Foot Fold Markers** with WS together and whip stitch all around to sandwich top and bottom together - adding a tiny amount of stuffing into the foot (not the leg) as you do so.

The leg will curl in on itself. Whip stitch the row ends together along the back of the leg.

Optional: You could add wire to the feet and legs to try and make the duck stand.

TO MAKE UP

Step 1: Ease and match the row ends of the two sides of the Breast and mattress stitch from the keel to the neck easing to make sure that the white band at the neck matches.

Step 2: With RS together, match the cast-on edge of the Left Wing with the cast-on edge of the Right Wing and back stitch just along the cast-on edges *(see fig. 7)*. Turn out to RS.

Step 3: With WS together, fold the tail in half at the **Tail Fold Markers**, matching **Tail to Keel Markers** *(see fig. 8)*, and mattress stitch to join each side of the tail.

Step 4: Working one side at a time, ease and match the Keel row ends with the Wing cast-off edge and row ends, matching the grey patch on the wing cast off to the **Tail to Keel Markers** *(see fig. 9)*, and mattress stitch together.

Step 5: Take time to stuff the duck though the gap at the tail and wing end, working the stuffing into each area and sculpting the body with your hands as you go.

Step 6: Match **Tail Markers** from both wing tips to the **Tail Marker** on the tail *(see fig. 10)*, then whip stitch to join from this point to the **Tail to Keel Markers**.

Note: Part of the black tail will lie beneath the wings.

Step 7: Finish stuffing, if needs be, through the remaining gap between the wings, then mattress stitch that last little seam to join the edges of the wings.

Step 8: Join the neck to the back with a stitch, so that the back of the neck lies against the tip of the triangle created at back *(see fig. 11)*.

Step 9: Finally, position the legs on the Keel as shown, and whip stitch around the cast-on edge.

10

11

Barn Owl

{Tyto alba}

———

Can the Barn Owl really be blamed for the weather? In olden days the Barn Owl was used to predict the weather by people in England. Apparently, a screeching owl meant cold weather, or a storm was coming. But it was also said "if heard during foul weather a change in the weather was at hand."

FINISHED SIZE

Approx. 20cm (8in) tall

YARN

You will need no more than one ball each of:

A: Drops Brushed Alpaca Silk in shade 19 curry

B: Drops Kid Silk in shade 15 dark brown

C: Drops Alpaca in shade 0618 light beige mix

D: Rico Essentials Super Kid Mohair Loves Silk in shade 001 white

E: Drops Flora in shade 02 white

F: Drops Brushed Alpaca Silk in shade 20 pink sand

G: Drops Baby Alpaca Silk in shade 2110 wheat (tiny amount for beak)

H: Drops Alpaca in shade 2923 goldenrod

I: Drops Kid Silk in shade 22 ash grey

Unless otherwise stated, multiple strands of yarn are used together throughout this pattern. The exact combinations of yarn to be used are indicated by multiple letters (see How to Use This Book).

NEEDLES

3.75 knitting needles

TENSION

15 rows and 11 stitches over 5cm (2in) with 3.75mm knitting needles

OTHER TOOLS AND MATERIALS

· 8 locking stitch markers

· 12mm black toy safety eyes

· Toy filling or yarn/fabric scraps

· A pair of wire bird legs and glue to attach the legs (see Tools and Materials)

BEGINNING WITH THE FACE

Owl's Left Side of Face

With yarn **ABC** cast on 23 sts for left side of owl's face.

Cut **A** and continue with yarn **BC** to create garter stitch ruffle.

Row 1(WS): K7, PM for left **Breast Marker**, k7, PM for left **Side Marker**, knit to end

Cut **BC** and join yarn **DDE**.

Row 2 (RS): Kfb, knit to end - 24sts

Row 3: Purl

Row 4: K10, k2tog, knit to last st, kfb

Row 5: Purl

Row 6: K10, k3tog, knit to end - 22sts

Row 7: Purl

Row 8: K9, k3tog, knit to end - 20sts

Row 9: Purl

Row 10: K9, cast off 7 sts, PM for left **Eye Marker** cast off remaining 4 sts - 9sts

With WS facing you, rejoin yarn **DDE** to remaining 9 sts.

Row 11: Purl

Work short rows (see General Techniques) to shape the brow:

Short row 1: K8, W+T

Short row 2: P8

Short row 3: K7, W+T

Short row 4: P7

Short row 5: K6, W+T

Short row 6: P6

Short row 7: K5, W+T

Short row 8: P5

Cast off 4 sts, PM for left **Eye Marker**, cast off remaining 5 sts.

Owl's Left Eye

With RS facing you, return to the **Eye Marker** on your right, with yarn **BF** pick up and knit 14 sts from **Eye Marker** to **Eye Marker** (see General Techniques).

Rows 1-3: Work 3 rows stocking stitch starting with a purl row

Cast off all left eye stitches.

Owl's Right Side of Face

With yarn **ABC** cast on 23 sts for right side of owl's face.

Cut **A** and continue with yarn **BC** to create garter stitch ruffle.

Row 1(WS): K9, PM for right **Side Marker**, k7, PM for right **Breast Marker**, knit to end

Cut **BC** and join yarn **DDE**.

Row 2(RS): Knit to last st, kfb - 24sts

Row 3: Purl

Row 4: Kfb, k11, k2tog, knit to end

Row 5: Purl

Row 6: K11, k3tog, knit to end - 22sts

Row 7: Purl

Row 8: K10, k3tog, knit to end - 20sts

Row 9: Purl

Row 10: Cast off 4 sts, PM for right **Eye Marker** cast off next 7 sts, knit to end - 9sts

Work short rows to shape the brow:

Short row 1: P8, W+T
Short row 2: K8
Short row 3: P7, W+T
Short row 4: K7
Short row 5: P6, W+T
Short row 6: K6
Short row 7: P5, W+T
Short row 8: K5
Row 11: Purl

Cast off 5 sts, PM for right **Eye Marker**, cast off remaining 4 sts.

Owl's Right Eye

With RS facing you, return to the **Eye Marker** on your right, with yarn **BF** pick up and knit 14 sts from **Eye Marker** to **Eye Marker**.

Rows 1-3: Work 3 rows stocking stitch starting with a purl row
Cast off all right eye stitches.

Join Inner Eye Seam

Working on one face side at a time, with RS together, fold the eye cast-off edge in half matching **Eye Marker** to **Eye Marker** and back stitch the cast-off edges together, followed by the two row ends *(see fig. 1, dotted line A to dotted line B)*. Then back stitch the white cast-off edges together.

Fit the toy eye at the centre of the eye (coloured part) and fasten in place.

Remove **Eye Markers**.

Join Left and Right Face

With WS together, match the two halves together along the row ends and with yarn **C** carefully whip stitch both sides together *(see fig. 2, dotted line A to dotted line B)*.

Then fold RS together, pinch the top of the head and work a few stitches to create a small dart to create the 'widow's peak'. When turned out to RS this will create a slight dip similar to the top of a heart.

Beak

With single strand of yarn **G**, work satin stitch over the straight part of the seam at the last 2cm (¾in) of the centre seam, then work two tiny stitches in **I** either side of the beak for nostrils.

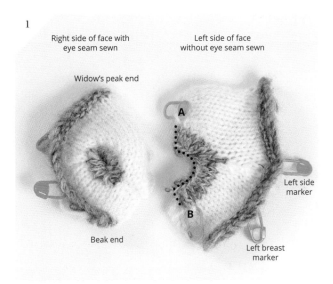

1

Right side of face with eye seam sewn

Left side of face without eye seam sewn

Widow's peak end

A

B

Left side marker

Beak end

Left breast marker

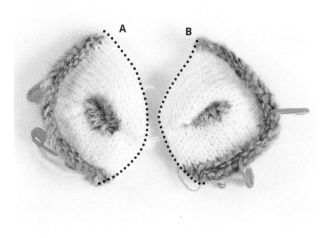

2

A   B

FRONT OF BODY AND LEGS

Breast

With RS facing you, return to owl's right side. With yarn **DDE** pick up and knit 14 sts from right **Breast Marker** to left **Breast Marker** from under the garter stitch ruffle at the lower face edge *(see fig. 3, dotted line A to B).*

Remove **Breast Markers**.

Row 1: Purl

Work short rows for right breast:

Short row 1: Cast on 7 sts, k11, W+T - 21sts

Short row 2: P11

Short row 3: K10, W+T

Short row 4: P10

Short row 5: K9, W+T

Short row 6: P9

Short row 7: K8, W+T

Short row 8: P8

Short row 9: Knit to end

Work short rows for left breast:

Short row 1: Cast on 7 sts, p11, W+T - 28sts

Short row 2: K11

Short row 3: P10, W+T

Short row 4: K10

Short row 5: P9, W+T

Short row 6: K9

Short row 7: P8, W+T

Short row 8: K8

Short row 9: Purl to end

Rows 2-7: Work 6 rows stocking stitch

Row 8: Kfb, k8, skpo, k6, k2tog, knit to last st, kfb

Row 9: Purl

Rows 10-17: Repeat last 2 rows four times

Row 18: K14, turn

Owl's Right Leg

Working on just these 14 sts for owl's right leg:

Row 1: P2tog, purl to end - 13sts

Row 2: Cast on 10 sts, PM for **Inner Leg Marker**, k10, PM for **Outer Leg Marker**, k2tog, k9, k2tog - 21sts

Row 3: Purl

Row 4: K2tog, k7, k2tog, k8, k2tog - 18sts

Row 5: Purl

Row 6: [K4, k2tog] 3 times - 15sts

Row 7: Purl

Row 8: [K3, k2tog] 3 times - 12sts

Row 9: Purl

Row 10: [K2, k2tog] 3 times - 9sts

Rows 11-15: Work 5 rows stocking stitch starting with a purl row

Cast off for talon end.

Owl's Left Leg

With RS facing you, rejoin yarn **BBE** to remaining 14 sts for left leg:

Row 1: K2tog, knit to end - 13sts

Row 2: Cast on 10 sts, PM for **Inner Leg Marker**, p10, PM for **Outer Leg Marker**, p2tog, p9, p2tog - 21sts

Row 3: Knit

Row 4: P2tog, p7, p2tog, p8, p2tog - 18sts

Row 5: Knit

Row 6: [P4, p2tog] 3 times - 15sts

Row 7: Knit

Row 8: [P3, p2tog] 3 times - 12sts

Row 9: Knit

Row 10: [P2, p2tog] 3 times - 9sts

Rows 11-15: Work 5 rows stocking stitch

Cast off purlwise for talon end.

Sewing Front of Body and Legs

Working on one side at a time match the corner from the 7 cast-on sts from the breast with the **Side Marker** and mattress stitch to join under the edge of the ruffle *(see fig. 4, dotted line, C to D).*

Working on one leg at a time, with WS together, fold leg in half across cast-off edge at talon end, match the **Inner Leg Marker** with the point where you divided for the legs and mattress stitch to join the leg seam down to the cast-off edge at talon end *(see fig. 5, dotted line A to dotted line B, and dotted line C to dotted line D).*

Remove **Inner Leg Markers**.

BACK OF HEAD AND BODY

Head Back

With yarn **ADI** cast on 24 sts for back of owl's head and neck.

PM at centre of cast-on edge for **Head Back Marker**.

Rows 1-6: Work 6 rows stocking stitch

Row 7: K10, kfb, k2, kfb, knit to end - 26sts

Row 8: Purl

Row 9: K11, kfb, k2, kfb, knit to end - 28sts

Row 10: Purl

Work short rows for top of the owl's head:

Short row 1: K27, W+T

Short row 2: P26, W+T

Short row 3: K25, W+T

Short row 4: P24, W+T

Short row 5: K23, W+T

Short row 6: P22, W+T

Short row 7: K21, W+T

Short row 8: P19, W+T

Short row 9: K18, W+T
Short row 10: P17, W+T
Short row 11: K16, W+T
Short row 12: P15, W+T
Short row 13: Knit to end
Cast off purlwise.

Back (Mantle)

With RS facing you, with yarn **AHI** pick up and knit 26 sts along the cast-off edge for neck part of owl's head.

PM at each end for **Primary Wing Markers**.

Row 1 (WS): Purl
Work short rows for owl's back:
Short row 1: K23, W+T
Short row 2: P20, W+T
Short row 3: K19, W+T
Short row 4: P18, W+T
Short row 5: K17, W+T
Short row 6: P16, W+T
Short row 7: K15, W+T
Short row 8: P14, W+T
Short row 9: K13, W+T
Short row 10: P12, W+T
Short row 11: Knit to end
Rows 2-4: Work 3 rows stocking stitch starting with a purl row
Cast off.

PM at centre of cast-off edge for **Wing Back Marker**.

Left Primary Wing

With RS of the back (mantle) facing you, return to owl's left. With yarn **BHI** pick up and knit 12 sts along the row ends and cast-off edge from the left **Primary Wing Marker** to the **Wing Back Marker** (*see fig. 6, dotted line*).

Row 1 (WS): Cast on 5 sts to extend the left wing, purl to end - 17sts
Row 2: Knit
Row 3: Pfb, purl to end - 18sts
Rows 4-6: Work 3 rows stocking stitch
Row 7: P2tog, purl to end - 17sts
Cut **BHI** and join yarn **DDE**.
Row 8: Knit
Row 9: P2tog, purl to end - 16sts
Cast off.

Right Primary Wing

With RS of the back (mantle) facing you, return to owl's right. With yarn **BHI** pick up and knit 12 sts along the cast-off edge and row ends, from the **Wing Back Marker** to the right **Primary Wing Marker**.

Row 1 (WS): Purl
Row 2: Cast on 5 sts to extend the right wing, knit to end - 17sts
Row 3: Purl to last st, pfb - 18sts
Rows 4-6: Work 3 rows stocking stitch
Row 7: Purl to last 2 sts, p2tog - 17sts
Cut **BHI** and join yarn **DDE**.
Row 8: Knit
Row 9: Purl to last 2 sts, p2tog - 16sts
Cast off.

Remove **Primary Wing Markers**.

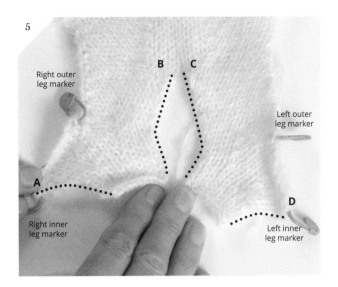

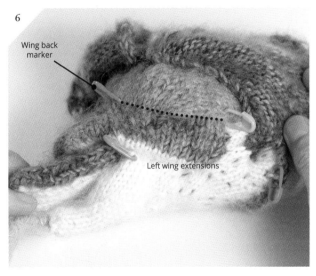

With RS together, match the cast-on edges of the wing extensions together. Back stitch to join along the cast-on edges.

Joining Head Back to Face

With WS together, match **Head Back Marker** to the top (widow's peak) of the centre seam of the face, and work a couple of mattress sts to join.

Then working on one side of the head at a time, match the corner of the head back cast-on to the **Side Marker**, carefully ease the edges together, then mattress stitch to join.

Remove **Side** and **Head Back Markers**.

TAIL

Underside of Tail

With RS facing you, return to the cast-on edges at the tops of the legs. With yarn **DDE** pick up and knit 24 sts from right **Outer Leg Marker** to left **Outer Leg Marker**.

Row 1: Purl
Row 2: K9, skpo, k2, k2tog, knit to end - 22sts
Row 3: Purl
Row 4: K8, skpo, k2, k2tog, knit to end - 20sts
Row 5: Purl
Row 6: K7, skpo, k2, k2tog, knit to end - 18sts
Row 7: Purl
Row 8: K6, skpo, k2, k2tog, knit to end - 16sts
Row 9: Purl
Row 10: K6, skpo, k2, k2tog, knit to end - 14sts
Row 11: Purl

Owl's Right Tail Feathers

Row 1: K7, turn
Working on just these 7 sts for owl's right tail feathers:
Row 2: P7, PM for **Fold Marker**
Cut **DDE** and join **ABC**.

Work short rows to shape the right side of tail:
Short row 1: K6, W+T
Short row 2: P6
Short row 3: K5, W+T
Short row 4: P5
Short row 5: K4, W+T
Short row 6: P4
Short row 7: K3, W+T
Short row 8: P3
Short row 9: K2, W+T
Short row 10: P2
Short row 11: K1, W+T
Short row 12: P1
Row 3-18: Work 16 rows stocking stitch
Cast off.

Owl's Left Tail Feathers

With RS facing you, rejoin yarn **DDE** to remaining 7 sts for left tail feathers:
Row 1: K7, PM for **Fold Marker**
Cut **DDE** and join **ABC**.

Work short rows to shape the left side of tail:

Short row 1: P6, W+T
Short row 2: K6
Short row 3: P5, W+T
Short row 4: K5
Short row 5: P4, W+T
Short row 6: K4
Short row 7: P3, W+T
Short row 8: K3
Short row 9: P2, W+T
Short row 10: K2
Short row 11: P1, W+T
Short row 12: K1
Rows 2-18: Work 17 rows stocking stitch starting with a purl row
Cast off.

Sewing the Tail Feathers

With RS together match the straight edges together and back stitch to join along the centre of the tail. Leave the shaped short-row section unsewn.

Fold the tail at the **Fold Markers**, the cast-off edges from both sides of the tail are then joined to the back (mantle) underneath the primary wings, with the end of the tail feathers centre seam matching to the **Wing Back Marker**. Whip stitch to join. The cast-off tail edges will be hidden by the primary wings.

Working on one side at a time, mattress stitch along the side of the tail to join outside to underside, from the tip to the **Outer Leg Marker**. The last four rows of the outside of the tail are then mattress stitched to the front of the body.

Remove **Fold**, **Wing Back**, and **Outer Leg Markers**.

Note: This leaves a gap on each side of the body, which will be closed by sewing down the primary wings.

Sewing the Primary Wings

Working on one side at a time, position the primary wings diagonally across the body from the breast to the top of the tail, aligning the back of each primary wing with the seam at the centre the tail.

The very tips of the wings should form a rounded 'W' shape on top of the tail. Whip stitch around the row ends and cast-off edge to join the wing to the body, tops of the legs, and the tail *(see fig. 7)*.

Stuff the owl's head, breast and legs, adding a tiny amount of stuffing in the tail, and at the owl's back, before completing the sewing on the second side.

SECONDARY WINGS

Note: The secondary wings are made separately and attached afterwards.

Owl's Left Wing

With yarn **ABC** cast on 5 sts.

Row 1 (RS): Kfb, k3, kfb - 7sts
Row 2: Purl
Row 3: Kfb, k5, kfb - 9sts
Row 4: Purl
Row 5: K2, kfb, k5, kfb - 11sts
Row 6: Purl
Row 7: K3, kfb, k6, kfb - 13sts
Row 8: Purl
Row 9: K1, kfb, k2, kfb, k7, kfb - 16sts
Row 10: Purl
Row 11: K2, kfb, k3, kfb, k8, kfb - 19sts
Row 12: Purl
Row 13: K3, kfb, k4, kfb, k9, kfb - 22sts
Row 14: Purl
Row 15: K4, kfb, k5, kfb, k10 kfb - 25sts
Rows 16-17: Work 2 rows stocking stitch starting with a purl row

Work short rows to shape the inside edges of the wing:

Short row 1: P11, W+T
Short row 2: K11
Short row 3: P10, W+T
Short row 4: K10
Short row 5: P9, W+T
Short row 6: K9
Short row 7: P8, W+T
Short row 8: K8
Row 18: Purl

Cut **BC** and join **DE** to work with yarn **ADE**.

Row 19: K2tog, knit to end - 24sts
Row 20: Purl to last 2 sts, p2tog - 23sts
Rows 21-22: Repeat last 2 rows once - 21sts

Cut **DE** and join **BC** to work with yarn **ABC**.

Row 23: K2tog, knit to end - 20sts
Row 24: Purl to last 2 sts, p2tog - 19sts
Rows 25-26: Repeat last 2 rows once - 17sts

Cut **BC** and join **DE** to work with yarn **ADE**.

Row 27: K2tog, knit to end - 16sts
Row 28: Purl to last 2 sts, p2tog - 15sts
Rows 29-30: Repeat last 2 rows once - 13sts

Cut **DE** and join **BC** to work with yarn **ABC**.

Row 31: K2tog, knit to end - 12sts
Row 32: Purl to last 2 sts, p2tog - 11sts
Row 33: K2tog, knit to last 2sts, k2tog - 9sts
Row 34: Purl to last 2 sts, p2tog - 8sts

Cut **BC** and join **DE** to work with yarn **ADE**.

Row 35: K2tog, knit to last 2sts, k2tog - 6sts
Row 36: Purl to last 2 sts, p2tog - 5sts
Row 37: K2tog, k1, k2tog - 3sts
Cut yarn, thread end through 3 sts, pull up and secure the end.

Owl's Right Wing

With yarn **ABC** cast on 5 sts.
Row 1 (RS): Kfb, k3, kfb - 7sts
Row 2: Purl
Row 3: Kfb, k5, kfb - 9sts
Row 4: Purl
Row 5: Kfb, k5, kfb, k2 - 11sts
Row 6: Purl
Row 7: Kfb, k6, kfb, k3 - 13sts
Row 8: Purl
Row 9: Kfb, k7, kfb, k2, kfb, k1 - 16sts
Row 10: Purl
Row 11: Kfb, k8, kfb, k3, kfb, k2 - 19sts
Row 12: Purl
Row 13: Kfb, k9, kfb, k4, kfb, k3 - 22sts
Row 14: Purl
Row 15: kfb, K10, kfb, k5, kfb, k4 - 25sts
Row 16: Purl
Work short rows to shape the inside edges of the wing:
Short row 1: K11, W+T
Short row 2: P11
Short row 3: K10, W+T
Short row 4: P10
Short row 5: K9, W+T
Short row 6: P9
Short row 7: K8, W+T
Short row 8: P8
Rows 17-18: Work 2 rows stocking stitch
Cut **BC** and join **DE** to work with yarn **ADE**.
Row 19: Knit to last 2 sts, k2tog - 24sts
Row 20: P2tog, purl to end - 23sts
Rows 21-22: Repeat last 2 rows once - 21sts
Cut **DE** and join **BC** to work with yarn **ABC**.
Row 23: Knit to last 2 sts, k2tog - 20sts
Row 24: P2tog, purl to end - 19sts
Rows 25-26: Repeat last 2 rows once - 17sts
Cut **BC** and join **DE** to work with yarn **ADE**.
Row 27: Knit to last 2 sts, k2tog - 16sts
Row 28: P2tog, purl to end - 15sts
Rows 29-30: Repeat last 2 rows once - 13sts
Cut **DE** and join **BC** to work with yarn **ABC**.
Row 31: Knit to last 2 sts, k2tog - 12sts
Row 32: P2tog, purl to end - 11sts
Row 33: K2tog, knit to last 2sts, k2tog - 9sts
Row 34: P2tog, purl to end - 8sts
Cut **BC** and join **DE** to work with yarn **ADE**.
Row 35: K2tog, knit to last 2sts, k2tog - 6sts
Row 36: P2tog, purl to end - 5sts
Row 37: K2tog, k1, k2tog - 3sts
Cut yarn, thread end through 3 sts, pull up and secure the end.
Weave in and neaten the yarn ends on both wings.

ATTACHING THE SECONDARY WINGS

Make sure you have the correct wing for the side of body (i.e. left wing for owl's left side, and right wing for owl's right side). Working with one wing at a time:

With RS of wing facing up, fit the cast-on edge from wing to the breast, halfway between the head cast-on edge and the start of the primary wing. Whip stitch to join along that cast-on edge.

Follow the line where the wing naturally sits over the back (mantle). Whip stitch to join along the shaped row ends and short row ends to join inside edge of wing to mantle. Stop stitching at the beginning of the first stripe.

Arrange the front edge of the wing so that it sits a little back from the edge of the primary wing. Whip stitch the row ends onto the primary wing. Stop stitching at the beginning of the first stripe.

Note: This seam will cause the wing to rise up a little. This is as intended.

FINISHING DETAILS FOR THE WINGS

When both wings have been sewn on, overlap the tips of the wings very slightly and whip stitch to join from the tips to the beginning of the last stripe.

TALONS

If using wire legs, brush them with glue then wrap double lengths of yarn **F** around and around the wire legs, finally push the wire legs (talons) into the body at the 'knitted legs' and whip stitch covered wire legs to knitted legs to secure in place.

If you don't want to use wire legs you can create yarn legs to tie over a branch. Work a running stitch around the cast-off edge of the legs and pull up to close the seam. Then with double lengths of yarn **F** stitch each of four claws into the fastened-off edge of each leg, to use to tie onto a branch.

BLACK DASHED FEATHER MARKINGS

With short lengths of yarn **I**, work random duplicate stitches over one half a stitch here and there over the breast. It's up to you how many or how few to do, all owls are different.

The owl will benefit from careful sculpting (see How to Use This Book) to enhance its shape.

Robin Redbreast

{Erithacus rubecula}

There are many ancient tales and myths
that tell of the reason how the robin got his
red breast but it's a fact that a robin should
never be harmed. Why? Why, it's a bird that
brought fire from Heaven, a holy bird and
loved by gardeners all over the world.

FINISHED SIZE

Approx. 14cm (5½in) long

YARN

You will need no more than one ball each of:

A: Drops Alpaca in shade 0601 dark brown

B: Drops Alpaca in shade 2925 rust mix

C: Drops Kid Silk in shade 33 rust

D: Drops Alpaca in shade 0618 light beige mix

E: Drops Alpaca in shade 2020 light camel mix

F: Drops Kid Silk in shade 15 dark brown

G: Drops Alpaca in shade 0100 off white

H: Drops Kid Silk in shade 10 grey

I: Rico Essentials Super Kid Mohair Loves Silk in shade 001 white

Unless otherwise stated, multiple strands of yarn are used together throughout this pattern. The exact combinations of yarn to be used are indicated by multiple letters (see How to Use This Book).

NEEDLES

2.5mm and 3mm knitting needles

TENSION

18 rows and 13 stitches over 5cm (2in) with 3mm knitting needles

OTHER TOOLS AND MATERIALS

· Safety pin for holding stitches

· 4mm brown or black toy safety eyes

· Toy filling or yarn/fabric scraps

BEGINNING WITH THE BEAK

With yarn **A** and 2.5mm needles cast on 1 st.

Note: Rows 1-6 will be worked as an i-cord (see General Techniques), so you will not turn the work between rows.

Row 1: Kfb, do not turn - 2sts

You can work over the tail end as you work the i-cord, or use a needle to thread the tail through the centre of the i-cord afterwards.

Row 2: Kfb, k1, do not turn - 3sts

Rows 3-5: work 3-stitch i-cord for 3 rows, do not turn

Row 6: Kfb, k1, kfb, do not turn - 5sts

HEAD

Cut **A** and join on yarn **BC**.

Row 7 (RS): K2, kfb, k2 - 6sts

Note: From now on you will be working back and forth.

Row 8 (WS): Purl

Row 9: K2, [kfb] twice, k2 - 8sts

Row 10: Purl

Cut **BC** and join on yarn **DEF**.

Row 11: [K1, kfb] four times - 12sts

Row 12: Purl

Work short rows (see General Techniques) to create the back of the head:

Short row 1: K10, W+T

Short row 2: P8, W+T

Short row 3: K7, W+T

Short row 4: P6, W+T

Short row 5: K5, W+T

Short row 6: P4, W+T

Short row 7: Knit to end

Row 13 (WS): Purl

Row 14: Cast on 3 sts, k5, kfb, k1, kfb, k2, [kfb, k1] twice, k1 - 19sts

Row 15: Cast on 3 sts, p10, p2tog, purl to end - 21sts

Row 16: Kfb, k7, skpo, k1, k2tog, knit to last st, kfb

Switch to the 3mm needles.

Work short rows to create the Back:

Short row 1: P20, W+T

Short row 2: K19, W+T

Short row 3: P18, W+T

Short row 4: K17, W+T

Short row 5: P16, W+T

Short row 6: K15, W+T

Short row 7: P14, W+T

Short row 8: K13, W+T

Short row 9: P12, W+T

Short row 10: K11, W+T

Short row 11: Purl to end

Row 17 (RS): K10, kfb, knit to end - 22sts

WINGS

Create a seam at the back by working on half of the stitches at a time:

Robin's Right Wing

Row 18 (WS): P11, turn

Rows 19-23: Working on just these 11 sts, work 5 rows of stocking stitch

Work short rows for Robin's Right Wing:

Short row 1: P10, W+T

Short row 2: K10

Short row 3: P9, W+T

Short row 4: K9

Short rows 5-18: Continue as set, working shorter and shorter rows, until…

Short row 19: P1, W+T,

Short row 20: K1

Row 24 (WS): [P2tog, p1] 3 times, p2 - 8sts

Row 25 (RS): Knit

Row 26: Cast off 5 sts purlwise, purl to end - 3sts

Cut yarns and leave these 3 sts on a small safety pin for the tail.

Robin's Left Wing

With WS facing you, rejoin yarn **DEF** ready to work the 11 sts for left wing.

Rows 18-24: Work 7 rows stocking stitch starting with a purl row

Work short rows for Robin's Left Wing:

Short row 1: K10, W+T

Short row 2: P10

Short row 3: K9, W+T

Short row 4: P9

Short rows 5-18: Continue as set, working shorter and shorter rows, until…

Short row 19: K1, W+T

Short row 20: P1

Row 25 (RS): [K2tog, k1] 3 times, k2 - 8sts

Row 26 (WS): Purl

TAIL

Row 27 (RS) first part: Cast off 5 sts, knit to end, do not turn - 3sts

Cut **E** and join on **A** to work with yarn **ADF**.

Row 27 (RS) second part: Slip the 3 sts held on the safety pin onto the RH needle, k3 - 6sts

Row 28 (WS): Purl

Row 29 (RS): Kfb, knit to last st, kfb - 8sts

Rows 30-46: Work 17 rows stocking stitch starting with a purl row

'V' shape at tail edge

Row 47 (RS): K4, turn, sl1 purlwise, p3, turn, k2, turn, sl1 purlwise, p1, turn, knit to end

Row 48: P4, turn, sl1 knitwise, k3, turn, p2, turn, sl1 knitwise, k1

Row 49: P3, p2tog, p3 - 7sts

Cut **A** to work with yarn **DF**, and switch to 2.5mm needles.

Rows 50-69: Work 20 rows of stocking stitch

Cut **D** and join on **G** to work with yarn **FG**.

Row 70 (RS): K3, kfb, knit to end - 8sts

Row 71: Purl

Row 72: Kfb, knit to last st, kfb - 10sts

Cut **F** and join on yarn **HI**, to work with yarn **GHI**, and switch to 3mm needles.

Rows 73-76: Repeat last 2 rows twice - 14sts

Row 77: Purl

Work short rows for Robin's Breast, left side:

Short row 1: K6, W+T

Short row 2: P6

Short row 3: K5, W+T

Short row 4: P5

Short rows 5-10: Continue as set, working shorter and shorter rows, until…

Short row 11: K1, W+T

Short row 12: P1

Row 78 (RS): Knit

Work short rows for Robin's Breast, right side:

Short row 1: P6, W+T

Short row 2: K6

Short row 3: P5, W+T

Short row 4: K5

Short rows 5-10: Continue as set, working shorter and shorter rows, until…

Short row 11: P1, W+T

Short row 12: K1

Row 79 (WS): P6, p2tog, purl to end - 13sts

RED BREAST

Join on yarn **BC** stranding yarns **GHI** behind the knitting until ready to work the upturned 'V' at the base of the red breast:

Row 80 (RS): K5 in **BC**, k3 in **GHI**, k5 in **BC**

Row 81 (WS): P6 in **BC**, p1 in **GHI**, p6 in **BC**

Cut **GHI** and continue to work with **BC**

Don't be concerned about all the loose ends - they make for perfect stuffing!

Row 82 (RS): K4, skpo, k1, k2tog, knit to end - 11sts

Row 83 (WS): Purl

Row 84: K3, skpo, k1, k2tog, knit to end - 9sts

Row 85: Purl

Row 86: K2, skpo, k1, k2tog, k2 - 7sts

Row 87: Purl

Row 88: K1, skpo, k1, k2tog, k1 - 5sts

Row 89: Purl

Row 90: Skpo, k1, k2tog - 3sts

Row 91: P3tog

Fasten off.

1

2

3

TO MAKE UP

Carefully press the knitting (first checking the yarn manufacturer's guidance about pressing).

With RS together, fold back in half and join the 'wing seam' created at row 17 with back stitch *(see fig. 1, dotted line)*.

With WS together, fold at the colour change at the tail.

Join *(See fig. 2)* to edge of beak by working a couple of stitches.

Along one side at a time, ease the row ends at the red breast to match with the head and mattress stitch stopping where the white part of the breast begins *(see fig. 3)*.

Fit the toy eyes in place referring to the photographs for placement.

Working on one side at a time, mattress stitch to join the top of the tail with the underside of the tail stopping the seam at the colour change for breast *(see fig. 4)*.

Tuck in all remaining yarn ends and stuff the robin's head and body through the open sides at the breast.

Note: The tail should remain un-stuffed.

Working on one side at a time carefully sew the white breast to the inside of the wings *(see fig. 5, dotted line)*.

Have the wings lying on top of the tail and mattress stitch the cast-off edges together *(see fig. 6, A to B)*.

Attach two lengths yarn **D** to just above the tail colour change so that you can attach the robin to a branch. The yarn will act as claws when you've tied them around, with three claws per leg.

Blue Tit

{Cyanistes caeruleus}

This most colourful of birds also has rich and colourful attributes. It is often regarded as a creature of nobility; it's a totem bird associated with the arrival of a bright future and the better things in life, of luck and happy relationships, of honour and family.

It's not surprising then that the blue tit only ever has just the one partner throughout the whole of its joyous life!

FINISHED SIZE

Approx. 11cm (4½in) long

YARN

You will need no more than one ball each of:

A: Drops Alpaca in shade 6205 light blue

B: Drops Kid Silk in shade 27 jeans blue

C: Drops Flora in shade 02 white

D: Rico Essentials Super Kid Mohair Loves Silk in shade 001 white

E: Drops Flora in shade 06 black

F: Drops Kid Silk in shade 10 grey

G: Drops Flora in shade 17 yellow

H: Rico Essentials Super Kid Mohair Loves Silk in shade 017 yellow

I: Drops Alpaca in shade 7238 dark olive mix

Unless otherwise stated, multiple strands of yarn are used together throughout this pattern. The exact combinations of yarn to be used are indicated by multiple letters (see How to Use This Book).

NEEDLES

2.5mm knitting needles

TENSION

19 rows and 15 stitches over 5cm (2in) with 2.5mm knitting needles

OTHER TOOLS AND MATERIALS

· 6 locking stitch markers

· 4mm black toy safety eyes

· Toy filling or yarn/fabric scraps

BEGINNING AT THE CREST

With yarn **AB** cast on 11 sts.

Row 1: Kfb, knit to last st, kfb - 13sts

Row 2: Purl

Cut **AB** and join **CD** to work with yarn **CD**.

Row 3: Kfb, knit to last st, kfb - 15sts

Row 4: Purl

Join yarn **EF** and carry yarn **CD** behind the next two rows.

Row 5: K7 in **EF**; then with **F**, cast on 3 sts (for beak) into next stitch, k2tog, cast off 2 sts; k7 to end in **EF**

Row 6: With yarn **EF**: P2tog, purl to last 2 sts, p2tog - 13sts

Note: In this section you will work with yarn **CD** and yarn **EF** in the same rows. The yarn not in use should be carried across the back of the work to the next place it is needed.

Row 7: Kfb, k4 in **CD**; k3 in **EF**; knit to last st, kfb in **CD** - 15sts

Row 8: P5 in **CD**; p5 in **EF**; purl to end in **CD**

Row 9: Skpo, k2 in **CD**; k7 in **EF**; k2, k2tog in **CD** - 13sts

Row 10: P3 in **CD**; p7 in **EF**; purl to end in **CD**

Cut **CD** and continue with yarn **EF**.

Rows 11-12: Work 2 rows stocking stitch

PM at each end of last row for **Neck Marker**.

Cut **EF** and join yarn **GH**.

Row 13: Kfb, knit to last st, kfb - 15sts

Work short rows (see General Techniques) to create the breast:

Short row 1: P14, W+T

Short row 2: K13, W+T

Short row 3: P14 to end.

Row 14: Kfb, knit to last st, kfb - 17sts

PM at each end of last row for **Breast Marker**.

Row 15: Purl

Rows 16-17: Repeat last 2 rows once - 19sts

Row 18: Kfb, k6, skpo, k1, k2tog, knit to last st, kfb

Row 19: Purl

Rows 20-21: Repeat last 2 rows once

Row 22: K7, skpo, k1, k2tog, knit to end - 17sts

Row 23: P2tog, purl to last 2 sts, p2tog - 15sts

Row 24: K5, skpo, k1, k2tog, knit to end - 13sts

PM at each end of last row for **Belly Marker**.

Row 25: Purl

Row 26: K4, skpo, k1, k2tog, knit to end - 11sts

Row 27: P4, p3tog, purl to end - 9sts

Row 28: Skpo, k5, k2tog - 7sts

Row 29: P2, p3tog, p2 - 5sts

TAIL UNDERSIDE

Cut **GH** and join yarn **AB**.

Rows 30-33: Work 4 rows stocking stitch

Row 34: Kfb, k3, kfb - 7sts

Rows 35-43: Work 9 rows stocking stitch starting with a purl row

Row 44: K3, turn, sl1, p2, turn, k2, turn, sl1, p1, turn, knit to end

Row 45: P3, turn, sl1, k2, turn, p2, turn, sl1, k1, turn, purl to end

UPPER TAIL

Cut **B** and join **F** to work with yarn **AF**.

Row 46: K3, kfb, k3 - 8sts

Rows 47-49: Work 3 rows stocking stitch starting with a purl row

Row 50: Skpo, knit to last 2 sts, k2tog - 6sts

Rows 51-61: Work 11 rows stocking stitch starting with a purl row

Cut **A** and join **E** to work with yarn **EF**.

Row 62: Kfb, knit to last st, kfb - 8sts

Row 63: Purl

Rows 64-67: Repeat last 2 rows twice - 12sts

Cast off.

WINGS

Carefully press the knitting (first checking the yarn manufacturer's guidance about pressing).

Note: To add the white detail to the wings, you will be alternating between yarn **AB** and **AD** in the same rows. This is done by swapping strands **B** and **D** and carrying the strand not in use across the back of the work to the next place it is needed.

Right Wing

With RS facing you and yarn **AB** pick up and knit 8 sts between right **Belly Marker** and right **Breast Marker** (see General Techniques).

Row 1: Purl to last 3 sts, pfb, p1, pfb - 10sts

Join **D**.

Row 2: Kfb, k5 in **AB**; k1 in **AD**; k3 in **AB** - 11sts

Row 3: P3 in **AB**; p1 in **AD**; purl to end in **AB**

Row 4: Kfb, k6 in **AB**; k1 in **AD**; k3 in **AB** - 12sts

Row 5: P2 in **AB**; p1 in **AD**; purl to end in **AB**

Row 6: Kfb, k8 in **AB**; k1 in **AD**; k2tog in **AB**

Row 7: P1 in **AD**; purl to end in **AB**

Cut **D**.

Row 8: Skpo, knit to last 2 sts, k2tog - 10sts

Row 9: Purl to last 2 sts, p2tog - 9sts

Cast off.

Left Wing

With RS facing you and yarn **AB** pick up and knit 8 sts between left **Breast Marker** and left **Belly Marker**.

Row 1: Pfb, p1, pfb, purl to end - 10sts

Join **D**.

Row 2: K3 in **AB**; k1 in **AD**; knit to last st, kfb in **AB** - 11sts

Row 3: P7 in **AB**; p1 in **AD**; purl to end in **AB**

Row 4: K3 in **AB**; k1 in **AD**; knit to last st, kfb in **AB** - 12sts

Row 5: P8 in **AB**; p1 in **AD**; purl to end in **AB**

Row 6: Skpo in **AB**; k1 in **AD**; knit to last st, kfb in AB

Row 7: P11 in **AB**; p1 in **AD**

Cut **D**.

Row 8: Skpo, knit to last 2 sts, k2tog - 10sts

Row 9: P2tog, purl to end - 9sts

Cast off.

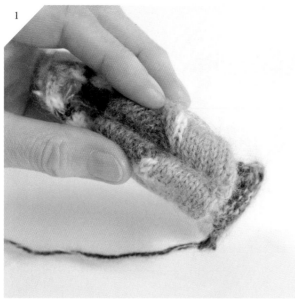

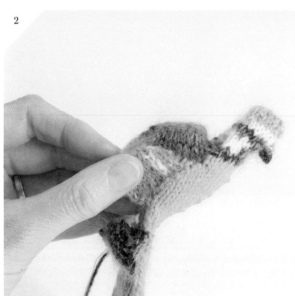

SEWING THE HEAD, TAIL, AND WINGS

With WS together, fold cast-on edge at the crest in half and mattress stitch the seam. Insert the eyes and secure. Tuck the yarn ends inside.

With WS together, fold the tail in half at the colour change that separates under tail from upper. Working on one side at a time, mattress stitch along each side edge. Then mattress stitch the body up to the **Belly Marker**.

Tuck yarn ends inside and match the cast-off edges from the wings and mattress stitch along just the cast-off edges to join (*see fig. 1*).

Remove **Belly Markers**.

BACK

Right Back

With RS facing you and yarn **HI**, pick up and knit 2 sts between right **Neck Marker** and right **Breast Marker**, then pick up a further 7 sts along the top of the right wing to the wing seam (*see fig. 2*) - 9sts.

Row 1 Purl

Work short rows to create right back:

Short row 1: K8, W+T

Short row 2: P8

Short row 3: K7, W+T

Short row 4: P7

Short row 5: Kfb, k5, W+T - 10sts

Short row 6: P7

Cast off.

Left Back

With RS facing you and yarn **HI**, pick up and knit 7 sts from wing seam along the top of the left wing to the left **Breast Marker**, then pick up and knit a further 2 sts up to the left **Neck Marker** - 9sts

Work short rows to create left back:

Short row 1: P8, W+T

Short row 2: K8

Short row 3: P7, W+T

Short row 4: K7

Short row 5: Pfb, p5, W+T - 10sts

Short row 6: K7

Cast off purlwise.

Match the cast-off edges of the left and right backs and mattress stitch to join.

Remove **Neck** and **Breast Markers**.

HEAD BACK

With RS facing you, with yarn **EF** pick up and knit 8 sts along the row ends at the top edge of the back, 4 sts on each side of the sewn seam *(see fig. 3)*.

Rows 1-2: Work 2 rows stocking stitch starting with a purl row

Rows 3: P2tog, purl to last 2 sts, p2tog - 6sts

Rows 4: [K2tog] 3 times - 3sts

Cast off purlwise.

Match the head back to the head front easing the edges together (you will need to tip the head front backwards), and whip stitch neatly together.

Tuck in all remaining yarn ends and stuff the blue tit's head and body through the gap under the wings, then whip stitch around the edges of the wing to join onto the tail *(see fig. 3)*.

Attach two lengths of yarn **A** to the yellow breast just above the tail (about 1cm (½in) from where the blue grey tail begins) so that you can attach the blue tit to a branch. The yarn will act as claws when you've tied the around, with three claws per leg.

3

Wolf

{Canis lupus}

Wolves are the bad and the good as conveyed in wolf folktales. It is aggressive, bloodthirsty and evil, and terrible consequences occur when associated with the full moon. However, there are also tales connected with its maternal instincts, its intelligence and respect for humans.

To be brought up by wolves would surely serve you well!

FINISHED SIZE

Approx. 37cm (14½in) tall, and 47cm (18½in) long

YARN

You will need no more than one ball each of:

A: Drops Alpaca in shade 0501 light grey mix

B: Drops Kid Silk in shade 01 off white

C: Drops Flora in shade 02 white

D: Drops Brushed Alpaca Silk in shade 04 light beige

E: Drops Brushed Alpaca Silk in shade 05 beige

F: Drops Kid Silk in shade 10 grey

G: Drops Alpaca in shade 0517 medium grey mix

H: Drops Brushed Alpaca Silk in shade 02 light grey

I: Drops Flora in shade 06 black

J: Drops Alpaca in shade 0618 light beige mix

K: James C Brett Faux Fur Chunky in shade H1 black/white

L: Drops Kid Silk in shade 15 dark brown (only a tiny amount)

Unless otherwise stated, multiple strands of yarn are used together throughout this pattern. The exact combinations of yarn to be used are indicated by multiple letters (see How to Use This Book).

NEEDLES

3.75mm and 5mm knitting needles

Optional: 3.75mm circular needle

TENSION

15 rows and 11 stitches over 5cm (2in) with 3.75mm knitting needles

14 rows and 9.5 stitches over 5cm (2in) with 5mm knitting needles

OTHER TOOLS AND MATERIALS

· 1 large safety pin or stitch holder

· 34 locking stitch markers

· 16mm orange or light brown toy safety eyes

· Toy filling or yarn/fabric scraps

BEGINNING AT THE MUZZLE

With yarn **ABC** and 3.75mm needles, cast on 13 sts.

PM at each end of last row for **Muzzle Marker**.

Row 1 (RS): Kfb, knit to last st, kfb - 15sts

Rows 2-4: Work 3 rows stocking stitch starting with a purl row

Row 5: Kfb, knit to last st, kfb - 17sts

Row 6: P2tog, purl to last 2 sts, p2tog - 15sts

Row 7: Cast off 5 sts, knit to last 5 sts, cast off last 5 sts and cut yarn - 5sts

BRIDGE OF THE NOSE

With WS facing you, with yarn **AEF** and 3.75mm needles, return to the remaining 5 sts.

Row 1 (WS): Pfb, purl to last st, pfb - 7sts

Row 2: K1, kfb, knit to last 2 sts, kfb, k1 - 9sts

Rows 3-5: Work 3 rows stocking stitch starting with a purl row

Row 6: K1, kfb, knit to last 2 sts, kfb, k1 - 11sts

Row 7: Pfb, purl to last st, pfb - 13sts

Row 8: K1, kfb, knit to last 2 sts, kfb, k1 - 15sts

Row 9: Purl

PM at each end of last row for **Nose Marker**.

Cut **E** and join **G** to work with yarn **AFG**.

Row 10: K2tog, knit to last 2 sts, k2tog - 13sts

Row 11: Purl

Rows 12-15: Repeat last 2 rows twice - 9sts

PM at each end of last row for **Bridge Marker**.

Cast off all 9 bridge sts.

FOREHEAD

With RS facing you, with yarn **AFG** and 3.75mm needles, pick up and knit 7 sts across bridge cast-off sts (see General Techniques).

Row 1: Purl

Row 2: Kfb, knit to last st, kfb - 9sts

Row 3: Purl

Row 4-7: Repeat last 2 rows twice - 13sts

Row 8: Kfb, k1, kfb, knit to last 3 sts, kfb, k1, kfb - 17sts

Row 9: Purl

Wolf's Left Eyebrow

Work short rows (see General Techniques) to create the wolf's left eyebrow:

Short row 1: Kfb, k2, W+T - 18sts

Short row 2: P4

Row 10: Knit

Wolf's Right Eyebrow

Work short rows to create the wolf's right eyebrow:

Short row 1: Pfb, p2, W+T - 19sts

Short row 2: K4

Row 11: Purl

PM at each end of last row for **Eye Edge Marker**.

Forehead

Row 12: Cast on 10 sts, PM for left **Temple Marker**, knit to end - 29sts

Row 13: Cast on 10 sts, PM for right **Temple Marker**, purl to end - 39sts

Cut **G** and join **B** to work with yarn **ABF**.

Work short rows to create the forehead:

Short row 1: K38, W+T

Short row 2: P37, W+T

Short row 3: K36, W+T

Short row 4: P35, W+T

Short row 5: K34, W+T

Short row 6: P33, W+T

Short row 7: PM for left **Ear Marker**, K33, PM for right **Ear Marker**, knit to end

Row 14: Purl

Work short rows to continue the forehead:

Short row 1: K29, W+T

Short row 2: P19, W+T

Short row 3: K18, W+T

Short row 4: P17, W+T

Short row 5: K16, W+T

Short row 6: P15, W+T

Short row 7: K14, W+T

Short row 8: P13, W+T

Short row 9: PM for left **Inner Ear Marker**, K13, PM for right **inner Ear Marker**, knit to end

Row 15: Purl

Cut yarn, leave all 39 head sts on a stitch holder.

WOLF'S LEFT CHEEK

With RS facing you, return to wolf's left nose and muzzle (on your right).

With yarn **BBC** and 3.75mm needles, pick up and knit 12 sts from wolf's left **Muzzle Marker** to wolf's left **Nose Marker**.

Row 1 (WS): Purl

Row 2: K3, k2tog, k1, k2tog, knit to end - 10sts

Row 3: Purl

Rows 4-5: Repeat last 2 rows once - 8sts

Row 6: Knit to last st, kfb - 9sts

Row 7: Purl

Rows 8-9: Repeat last 2 rows once - 10sts

Work short rows to create the wolf's left cheek:

Short row 1: K9, W+T

Short row 2: P9

Short row 3: K8, W+T

Short row 4: P8

PM at end of last row for **Jaw Marker**.

Cut **C** and join **H** to work with yarn **BBH**.

Row 10: K10, pick up and knit 8 sts along to wolf's left **Nose Marker** - 18sts

Rows 11-16: Work 6 rows stocking stitch starting with a purl row

Row 17: [P2tog twice, purl to end - 16sts

Cut **H** and join **E** to work with yarn **BBE**.

Row 18: Knit

PM at end of last row for **Eye Corner Marker**.

Row 19: Cast off 4 sts purlwise, purl to end - 12sts

Row 20: Knit to last 2 sts, k2tog - 11sts

Row 21: P2tog, purl to end - 10sts

Row 22: Knit

PM at end of last row for **Eye Marker**.

Work short rows to create the top of the wolf's temple:

Short row 1: P7, W+T

Short row 2: K7

Short row 3: P6, W+T

Short row 4: K6

Short row 5: P5, W+T

Short row 6: K5

Short row 7: P4, W+T

Short row 8: K4

Rows 23-24: Work 2 rows stocking stitch starting with a purl row

PM at end of last row for **Temple Marker**.

Cast off all 10 Temple sts purlwise.

Add Colour to the Wolf's Left Eyebrow

With RS facing you, return to wolf's left eye (on your right).

With yarn **BBE** and 3.75mm needles, pick up and knit 9 sts from wolf's left **Bridge Marker** to wolf's left **Eye Edge Marker**.

Row 1 (WS): P2tog, purl to end - 8sts

Row 2: K2tog, knit to end - 7sts

Cast off purlwise. Weave in ends to neaten.

WOLF'S RIGHT CHEEK

With RS facing you, return to wolf's right nose and muzzle (on your left).

With yarn **BBC** and 3.75mm needles, pick up and knit 12 sts from wolf's right **Nose Marker** to wolf's right **Muzzle Marker**.

Row 1 (WS): Purl

Row 2: K4, k2tog, k1, k2tog, knit to end - 10sts

Row 3: Purl

Row 4: K2, k2tog, k1, k2tog, knit to end - 8sts

Row 5: Purl

Row 6: Kfb, knit to end - 9sts

Rows 7-8: Repeat last 2 rows once - 10sts

Work short rows to create the wolf's right cheek:

Short row 1: P9, W+T

Short row 2: K9

Short row 3: P8, W+T

Short row 4: K8

PM at end of last row for **Jaw Marker**.

Cut **C** and join **H** to work with yarn **BBH**.

Row 9: Purl 10, pick up and purl 8 sts along to wolf's right **Nose Marker** - 18sts

Rows 10-15: Work 6 rows stocking stitch

Row 16: [K2tog] twice, knit to end - 16sts

Cut **H** and join **E** to work with yarn **BBE**.

Row 17: Purl

PM at end of last row for **Eye Corner Marker**.

Row 18: Cast off 4 sts, knit to end - 12sts

Row 19: Purl to last 2 sts, p2tog - 11sts

Row 20: K2tog, knit to end - 10sts

Row 21: Purl

PM at end of last row for **Eye Marker**.

Work short rows to create the top of the wolf's temple:

Short row 1: K7, W+T

Short row 2: P7

Short row 3: K6, W+T

Short row 4: P6

Short row 5: K5, W+T

Short row 6: P5

Short row 7: K4, W+T

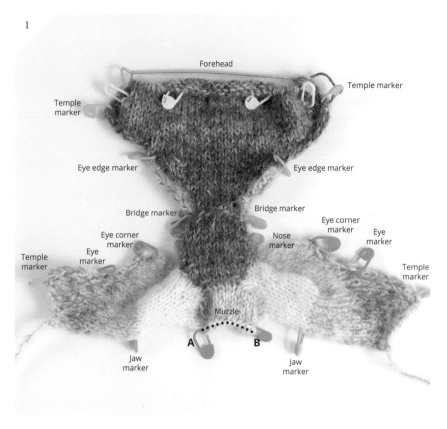

1

Forehead

Temple marker

Temple marker

Eye edge marker

Eye edge marker

Bridge marker

Bridge marker

Eye corner marker

Eye corner marker

Eye marker

Nose marker

Eye marker

Temple marker

Eye marker

Temple marker

Muzzle

A   B

Jaw marker

Jaw marker

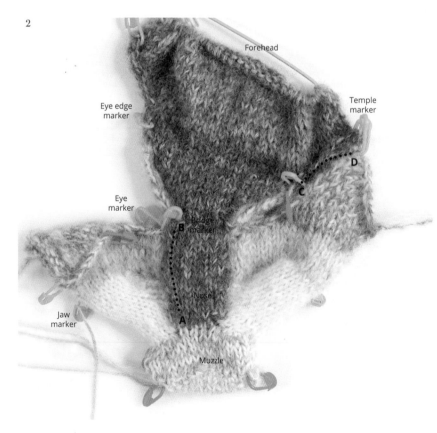

2

Forehead

Eye edge marker

Temple marker

Eye marker

D

C

Bridge marker

B

Nose

A

Jaw marker

Muzzle

Short row 8: P4

Rows 22-23: Work 2 rows stocking stitch

PM at end of last row for **Temple Marker**.

Cast off all 10 Temple sts.

Add Colour to the Wolf's Right Eyebrow

With RS facing you, return to wolf's right eye (on your left).

With yarn **BBE** and 3.75mm needles, pick up and knit 9 sts from wolf's right **Eye Edge Marker** to wolf's right **Bridge Marker**.

Row 1 (WS): Purl to last 2 sts, p2tog - 8sts

Row 2: Knit to last 2, k2tog - 7sts

Cast off purlwise. Weave in ends to neaten *(see fig. 1, marker placement)*.

SEWING NOSE SEAM

Working on one side of the face at a time, match the **Eye Corner Marker** with the **Bridge Marker** and mattress stitch to join along the side of the bridge of the nose from **Eye Corner Marker** along to the **Nose Marker** *(see fig. 2, dotted line from A to B)*.

Remove **Eye Corner**, **Bridge**, and **Nose Markers**.

Working on one side of the forehead at a time, match the **Temple Markers** together, then match the **Eye Edge Marker** with the **Eye Marker** and ease the seam together (you may find it easier if you pin before sewing). Mattress stitch from the **Temple Marker** to the **Eye Marker** *(see fig. 2, dotted line from C to D)*.

Remove **Eye** and **Eye Edge Markers**.

CHIN AND THROAT

With RS facing you, return to the cast-on edge at the muzzle from the beginning of the pattern.

With yarn **BCD** and 3.75mm needles, pick up and knit 12 sts across the cast-on edge from wolf's **Right Muzzle Marker** to **Left Muzzle Marker** *(see fig. 3, dotted line from A to B)*.

Work short rows to create wolf's chin:

Short row 1: P7, W+T

Short row 2: K2, W+T

Short row 3: P3, W+T

Short row 4: K4, W+T

Short row 5: P5, W+T

Short row 6: K6, W+T

Short row 7: P7, W+T

Short row 8: K8, W+T

Short row 9: Purl to end
Rows 1-8: Work 8 rows stocking stitch
PM at each end of last row for **Throat Markers**.
Rows 9-14: Work 6 rows stocking stitch
Cut **BCD**, change to 5mm needles and join yarn **K**.
Row 15: Kfb, knit to last st, kfb - 14sts
Row 16: Purl
Rows 17-18: Repeat last 2 rows once - 16sts
Rows 19-32: Work 14 rows stocking stitch
PM at each end of last row for Fur Markers.

BREAST AND BELLY

Cut **K** and join yarn **BCD**.
Rows 33-38: Work 6 rows stocking stitch
Row 39: Kfb, knit to last st, kfb - 18sts
Rows 40-55: Work 16 rows stocking stitch starting with a purl row
PM at each end of last row for **Breast Markers**.
Rows 56-66: Work 11 rows stocking stitch starting with a purl row
PM at each end of last row for **Belly Markers**.
Rows 67-82: Work 16 rows stocking stitch
Row 83: K2tog, knit to last 2 sts, k2tog - 16sts
Row 84: Purl
Rows 85-96: Repeat last 2 rows 6 times - 4sts
Rows 97-102: Work 6 rows stocking stitch
PM at each end of last row for **Inner Thigh Markers**.
Cast off for tail end.

NECK

With RS facing you, with yarn **DFG** and 3.75mm needles, pick up and knit 14 sts from left **Jaw Marker** along row ends and cast-off edge to left **Temple Marker** (see fig. 4, dotted line from A to B), pick up and knit 3 sts along row ends, slip the 39 head stitches from the stitch holder onto LH knitting needle, k39, pick up and knit 3 sts along row ends to right **Temple Marker**, pick up and knit 14 sts to wolf's right **Jaw Marker** - 73sts
Note: You might find this step easier with a circular needle.
Remove **Temple Markers**.
Row 1: Purl
Row 2: K13, k2tog, k11, k2tog, k5, skpo, k3, k2tog, k5, k2tog, k11, k2tog, knit to end - 67sts
Row 3: Purl
Cut **D** and join **E** to work with **EFG**.
Row 4: K13, k2tog, k9, k2tog, k4, skpo, k3, k2tog, k4, k2tog, k9, k2tog, knit to end - 61sts
Row 5: Purl
Row 6: K13, k2tog, k7, k2tog, k3, skpo, k3, k2tog, k3, k2tog, k7, k2tog, knit to end - 55sts
Row 7: Purl
Row 8: K13, k2tog, k5, k2tog, PM for left **Ear Back Marker**, k2, skpo, k3, k2tog, k2, PM for right **Ear Back Marker**, k2tog, k5, k2tog, knit to end - 49sts
Row 9: Purl
Cut **EFG**, change to 5mm needles and join yarn **K**.

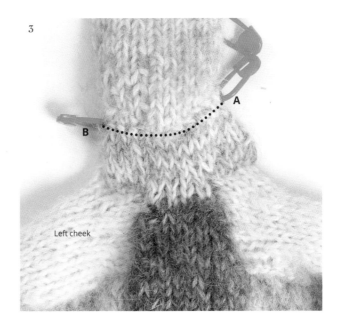

3

Left cheek

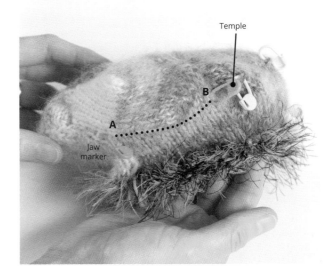

4

Temple

A

B

Jaw marker

Row 10: K13, k2tog, k3, k2tog, k1, skpo, k3, k2tog, k1, k2tog, k3, k2tog, knit to end - 43sts

Row 11: Purl

Row 12: K15, k2tog, k1, skpo, k3, k2tog, k1, k2tog, knit to end - 39sts

Row 13: Purl

Row 14: Kfb, knit to last st, kfb - 41sts

Row 15: Purl

Rows 16-19: Repeat last 2 rows twice - 45sts

PM at each end of last row for **Neck Marker**.

Rows 20-33: Work 14 rows stocking stitch

Cut **K** and join yarn **AEG**.

Row 34: Kfb, knit to last st, kfb - 47sts

Row 35: Purl

Rows 36-39: Repeat last 2 rows twice - 51sts

Rows 40-43: Work 4 rows stocking stitch

Row 45: Cast on 6 sts, PM for left **Front Marker** knit to end - 57sts

Row 45: Cast on 6 sts, PM for right **Front Marker**, purl to end - 63sts

Row 46: K27, skpo, k5, k2tog, knit to end - 61sts

Row 47: Purl

Row 48: K27, skpo, k3, k2tog, knit to end - 59sts

Row 49: Purl

Row 50: K27, skpo, k1, k2tog, knit to end - 57sts

Row 51: Purl

Row 52: K2tog, k24, skpo, k1, k2tog, knit to last 2 sts, k2tog - 53sts

Row 53: Purl

Row 54: K2tog, k22, skpo, k1, k2tog, knit to last 2 sts, k2tog - 49sts

Row 55: Purl

Row 56: K2tog, k20, skpo, k1, k2tog, knit to last 2 sts, k2tog - 45sts

Row 57: Purl

Row 58: Cast off 8 sts for **Side Seam**, knit to end - 37sts

Row 59: Cast off 8 sts for **Side Seam**, purl to end - 29sts

Row 60: Cast on 6 sts for **Side Seam**, knit to end - 35sts

Row 61: Cast on 6 sts for **Side Seam**, purl to end - 41sts

Rows 62-71: Work 10 rows stocking stitch

HIND LEGS - UPPER PART

Row 72: Cast on 10 sts for wolf's left hind leg, PM for left **Upper Thigh Marker**, knit to end - 51sts

Row 73: Cast on 10 sts for wolf's right hind leg, PM for right **Upper Thigh Marker**, purl to end - 61sts

Work short rows to create the top of the left leg:

Short row 1: K11, W+T

Short row 2: P1, W+T

Short row 3: K2, W+T

Short row 4: P3, W+T

Short row 5: K4, W+T

Short rows 6-19: Continue as set, working longer rows each time until…

Short row 20: P19, W+T

Short row 21: Knit to end

Work short rows to create the top of the right leg:

Short row 1: P11, W+T

Short row 2: K1, W+T

Short row 3: P2, W+T

Short row 4: K3, W+T

Short row 5: P4, W+T

Short rows 6-19: Continue as set, working longer rows each time until…

Short row 20: K19, W+T

Short row 21: Purl to end

Row 74: K2tog, knit to last 2 sts, k2tog - 59sts

Row 75: Purl

Rows 76-81: Repeat last 2 rows three times - 53sts

Cut **G** and join **J** to work with yarn **AEJ**.

Row 82: K2tog, k21, skpo, k3, k2tog, knit to last 2 sts, k2tog - 49sts

Row 83: Purl

Row 84: K2tog, k19, skpo, k3, k2tog, knit to last 2 sts, k2tog - 45sts

Row 85: Purl

Row 86: K2tog, k17, skpo, k3, k2tog, knit to last 2 sts, k2tog - 41sts

Row 87: Purl

Row 88: K2tog, k15, skpo, k3, k2tog, knit to last 2 sts, k2tog - 37sts

Row 89: Purl

Row 90: K2tog, k13, skpo, k3, k2tog, knit to last 2 sts, k2tog - 33sts

Row 91: Purl

Row 92: K2tog, k11, skpo, k3, k2tog, knit to last 2 sts, k2tog - 29sts

Row 93: Purl

Row 94: K2tog, k5, k2tog, k2, skpo, k3, k2tog, k2, k2tog, knit to last 2 sts, k2tog - 23sts

Row 95: Purl

Row 96: K2tog, k3, k2tog, k1, skpo, k3, k2tog, k1, k2tog, knit to last 2 sts, k2tog - 17sts

Row 97: Purl

PM at each end of last row for **Tail Markers**.

TAIL

Cut **AEJ** and join yarn **K**.

Rows 1-20: Work 20 rows stocking stitch

Row 21: K2tog, knit to last 2 sts, k2tog - 15sts

Row 22: Purl

Rows 23-32: Repeat last 2 rows five times - 5sts

PM at each end of last row for **Tail Fold Markers**.

Row 33: Knit

Row 34: Purl

Row 35: Kfb, knit to last st, kfb - 7sts

Rows 36-43: Repeat last 2 rows four times - 15sts

Rows 44-54: Work 11 rows stocking stitch starting with a purl row

Row 55: K2tog, knit to last 2 sts, k2tog - 13sts

Rows 56-58: Work 3 rows stocking stitch starting with a purl row

Row 59: K2tog, knit to last 2 sts, k2tog - 11sts

Rows 60-62: Work 3 rows stocking stitch starting with a purl row

Row 63: K2tog, knit to last 2 sts, k2tog - 9sts

Cast off.

Wolf's Left Inner Thigh

With RS facing you, with yarn **BCJ** and 5mm needles, pick up and knit 26 sts across row ends from wolf's left **Inner Thigh Marker** to wolf's left **Belly Marker** (*see fig. 6, dotted line from A to B*).

Rows 1-5: Work 5 rows stocking stitch starting with a purl row

PM at end of last row for **Inner Tail Marker**.

Row 6: K2tog, knit to last st, kfb

Row 7: Purl

Rows 8-11: Repeat last 2 rows twice

Row 12: K2tog twice, k18, k2tog twice - 22sts

PM at end of last row for **Inner Upper Thigh Marker**.

Cast off all front of inner thigh sts purlwise.

Wolf's Right Inner Thigh

With RS facing you, with yarn **BCJ** and 5mm needles, pick up and knit 26 sts across row ends from wolf's right **Belly Marker** to wolf's right **Inner Thigh Marker**.

Rows 1-4: Work 4 rows stocking stitch starting with a purl row PM at end of last row for **Inner Tail Marker**.

Row 5: Purl

Row 6: Kfb, knit to last 2 sts, k2tog

Row 7: Purl

Rows 8-11: Repeat last 2 rows twice

Row 12: [K2tog] twice, k18, [k2tog] twice - 22sts PM at start of last row for **Inner Upper Thigh Marker**.

Cast off all front of inner thigh sts purlwise.

Remove **Inner Thigh Markers**.

NECK AND BODY SEAMS

Jaw Seam

Working on one side at a time, with RS together, match the **Jaw Marker** with the **Throat Marker** and back stitch from the **Muzzle Marker** to the **Jaw Marker**. Turn out to RS. *(see fig. 5, dotted line)*

Remove **Muzzle** and **Throat Markers**.

Join Side Seams

Working on one side of the body at a time, with RS together, match the **Side Seam** cast-off edge with the **Side Seam** cast-on edge and back stitch. Turn out to RS.

Join Inner to Outer Thigh

Note: You may find it easier if you pin each of these seams before sewing.

Working on one side at a time, with RS together match the end of the **Side Seam** with the **Belly Marker,** then match the **Upper Thigh Marker** with the **Inner Upper Thigh Marker**. Ease together and back stitch from the **Side Seam** to the **Upper Thigh Marker** *(see fig. 6)*.

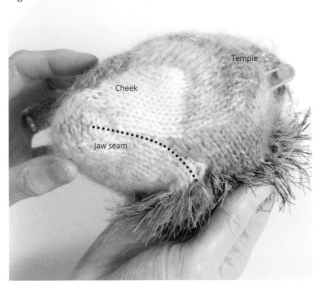

5

Temple

Cheek

Jaw seam

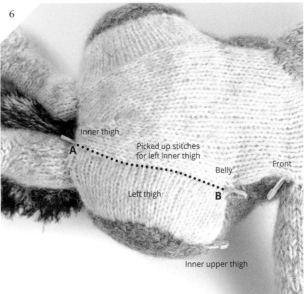

6

Inner thigh

Picked up stitches for left inner thigh

A

Belly

Front

Left thigh

B

Inner upper thigh

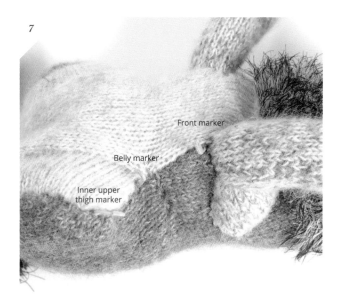

Front marker

Belly marker

Inner upper thigh marker

Remove **Belly**, **Upper Thigh** and **Inner Upper Thigh Markers**.

Now match the **Tail Marker** with the **Inner Tail Marker** and ease together, then back stitch from the end of the previous seam to the **Tail Marker**. Turn out to RS.

Remove **Inner Tail Markers**.

Join Neck and Jaw

Working on one side at a time, match **Neck Marker** with the **Fur Marker** and ease together. Mattress stitch from the **Jaw Marker** to the **Neck Marker**.

Remove **Jaw** and **Fur Markers**.

Join Front to Breast

Working on one side at a time, match the **Front Marker** with the **Breast Marker** and ease together. Mattress stitch from the **Neck Marker** to the **Front Marker**.

Remove **Neck** and **Breast Markers**.

Stuff the Head

Tuck in yarn ends and stuff the head, but not too much. The shaping around the muzzle and at the sides of the nose are meant to be quite soft, not firm and bulging.

Join Front to Belly

Working on one side at a time, mattress stitch from the **Side Seam** to the **Front Marker** *(see fig. 7)*.

Remove **Front Markers**.

Stuff the Body

Tuck in yarn ends and stuff the body through the opening at the tail end, making sure the stuffing fills out the upper thigh shaping nicely, but not over stuffing.

Tail Seams

Fold tail at the **Tail Fold Markers** with WS together. Match the cast-off edge of the tail to the stitches between the two **Tail Markers**, then whip stitch to join along the tail sides. The tail is not stuffed.

Remove **Tail Fold** and **Tail Markers**.

EYES (MAKE TWO ALIKE)

With yarn **II** and 3.75mm needles, cast on 7 sts.

Rows 1-6: Work 6 rows stocking stitch
Cast off.

Sewing the eyes

With RS together, fold each eye in half at the row ends, cast-on edge to cast-off edge.

Working on one side at a time whip stitch along the row ends. Turn out to RS and open out into an almond-like shape with the seamed ends tucked underneath.

Attach the toy eye in the centre of the knitted eye then insert the knitted eye into the left eye socket (*see fig. 8*). Using yarn **E** carefully whip stitch around the eye to join it into the eye socket.

NOSE

With yarn **IIL** and 3.75mm needles, cast on 10 sts.

Rows 1-4: Work 4 rows stocking stitch
Row 5: [K2tog, k2] twice, k2tog - 7sts
Row 6: Purl
PM at each end for **Nose Fold Markers**.
Cut **L** to work with yarn **II**.
Row 7: Cast on 4 sts, knit to end - 11sts
Row 8: Cast on 4 sts, purl to end - 15sts
Rows 9-10: Work 2 rows stocking stitch
Cast off.

Sewing on the nose

Working on one side at a time, with RS together, fold nose at the **Nose Fold Markers**, matching row end of initial cast-on with row end of cast-off. Back stitch to join row ends between initial cast-on and **Nose Fold Marker**, to cast-on edge (from Rows 7 or 8) and row ends before cast-off. Turn out to RS, and stuff the nose a little with yarn **I**.

Remove **Nose Fold Markers**.

Fit the nose over the beige muzzle (*see fig. 9*) and whip stitch in place. The cast-on edge from beginning of nose becomes the top of the nose, the cast-off edge lies at the mouth seam.

EARS (MAKE TWO ALIKE)

Outer Ear

With yarn **DFG** and 3.75mm needles, cast on 21 sts for the base of the ear.

Row 1 (WS): Purl
Row 2: Kfb, knit to last st, kfb - 23sts
Cut **DG** and join **EI** to work with yarn **EFI**.

Rows 3-9: Work 7 rows stocking stitch starting with a purl row
Row 10: K9, skpo, k1, k2tog, knit to end - 21sts
Row 11: Purl
Row 12: K8, skpo, k1, k2tog, knit to end - 19sts
Row 13: Purl
Row 14: K7, skpo, k1, k2tog, knit to end - 17sts
Row 15: P3, p2tog, p7, p2tog, purl to end - 15sts
Row 16: K5, skpo, k1, k2tog, knit to end - 13sts
Row 17: [P3, p2tog] twice, purl to end - 11sts
Row 18: K3, skpo, k1, k2tog, knit to end - 9sts
Row 19: P3, p3tog, purl to end - 7sts
Row 20: K2tog, k3, k2tog - 5sts
Cut yarn, thread end through all 5 stitches for ear peak.

Inner Ear

With RS facing you, with yarn **II** and 3.75mm needles, and beginning at the base of the ear, pick up and knit 20 sts (10 sts either side of the ear peak) all around the outer edge of the outer ear, working from ear base on side one to ear peak to ear base on side two.

Row 1 (WS): Purl
Cut **II** and join yarn **BD**.

Work short rows to shape the inner ear - side one:

Short row 1: K9, W+T
Short row 2: P9
Short row 3: K8, W+T
Short row 4: P8
Short row 5: K7, W+T
Short row 6: P7
Row 2: Cast off 10 sts, knit to end

Work short rows to shape the inner ear - side two:

Short row 1: P9, W+T
Short row 2: K9
Short row 3: P8, W+T
Short row 4: K8
Short row 5: P7, W+T
Short row 6: K7

Cast off 10 sts purlwise.

With WS together, flatten the inner ear down to lay inside the outer ear and carefully whip stitch around the cast-off edges and along the row ends of the inner ear so joining to the outer ear.

Attach Ears to Head

Working on one ear at a time place the base of the ear onto the head so that the front corners of the ear 'triangle' match with the **Ear Marker** and **Inner Ear Markers**, and the centre of the ear base matches with the **Ear Back Marker** *(see fig. 10)*, then whip stitch neatly and securely to join ear to head.

When you've joined the ear back, pull the ear inner onto the head and whip stitch that in place too.

Remove **Ear**, **Inner Ear**, and **Ear Back Markers**.

WOLF'S LEFT FORELEG

With yarn **BCDJ** and 5mm needles, cast on 10 sts for top of left foreleg shoulder.

Row 1 (RS): Kfb, knit to last st, kfb - 12sts
Row 2: Purl
Rows 3-4: Repeat last 2 rows once - 14sts
Rows 5-8: Work 4 rows stocking stitch
Row 9 (RS): K2tog, knit to last 2 sts, k2tog - 12sts
Row 10: Purl
Rows 11-12: Repeat last 2 rows once - 10sts
Row 13: Cast on 10 sts for back of left foreleg, knit to end - 20sts
Rows 14-48: Work 35 rows stocking stitch starting with a purl row

Wolf's Left Front Paw

Row 49: K8, kfb, k2, kfb, knit to end - 22sts
Row 50: Purl
Row 51: K9, kfb, k2, kfb, knit to end - 24sts
Row 52: Purl
Row 53: K10, kfb, k2, kfb, knit to end - 26sts
Row 54: Purl

Work short rows for wolf's front paw:

Short row 1: K21, W+T
Short row 2: P16, W+T
Short row 3: K15, W+T
Short row 4: P14, W+T
Short row 5: K13, W+T
Short row 6: P12, W+T
Short row 7: K11, W+T
Short row 8: P10, W+T
Short row 9: K9, W+T
Short row 10: P8, W+T
Short row 11: Knit to end

Cast off purlwise.

WOLF'S RIGHT FORELEG

With yarn **BCDJ** and 5mm needles, cast on 10 sts for top of right foreleg shoulder.

Rows 1-12: Work as for **Wolf's Left Foreleg Rows 1-12**

Row 13: Knit

Row 14: Cast on 10 sts for back of right foreleg, purl to end - 20sts

Rows 15-48: Work 34 rows stocking stitch

Wolf's Right Front Paw

Work as for **Wolf's Left Front Paw**.

Working on one foreleg at a time at a time, with WS together fold the cast-off edge in half and mattress stitch to join along the bottom of the paw.

Mattress stitch to join the row ends for the back of the leg, a stuff fairly firmly through the cast-on edge.

Whip stitch around the cast-on edge to join leg part of foreleg to the body over the 'front' cast-on section just beneath the fur at the neck and at the seam that joins the back to breast. Add a little bit of stuffing just to pad out the 'shoulder' a little.

WOLF'S HIND FOOT (MAKE TWO ALIKE)

With yarn **BCDJ** and 5mm needles, cast on 10 sts for leg part of the foot.

Rows 1-10: Work 10 rows stocking stitch

Row 11: Cast on 20 sts for top of foot side one, knit to end - 30sts

Rows 12-14: Work 3 rows stocking stitch starting with a purl row

Work short rows to shape foot pad - side one:

Short row 1: K13, W+T
Short row 2: P13
Short row 3: K12, W+T
Short row 4: P12
Short row 5: K11, W+T
Short row 6: P11
Short row 7: K10, W+T
Short row 8: P10

Rows 15-30: Work 16 rows stocking stitch

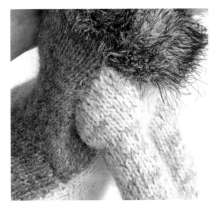

Work short rows to shape foot pad - side two:

Short row 1: K13, W+T
Short row 2: P13
Short row 3: K12, W+T
Short row 4: P12
Short row 5: K11, W+T
Short row 6: P11
Short row 7: K10, W+T
Short row 8: P10

Rows 31-32: Work 2 rows stocking stitch

Row 33: Cast off 20 sts for top of foot side two, knit to end - 10sts

Rows 34-43: Work 10 rows stocking stitch starting with a purl row

Cast off all sts for top of leg part of foot.

With WS together, fold foot in half matching initial cast-on edge to final cast-off edge, and mattress stitch from this edge down to the top of the foot, along the top of the foot, and down the row ends to the fold.

Mattress stitch the remaining row ends for the back of foot.

Stuff fairly firmly through the open edge at the leg part of the foot.

Whip stitch around the open edge to join leg part of foot to the body at thigh.

With yarn **J** work four straight stitches over the feet, pulling each stitch so that it draws the stuffed paw inwards to create a toe-divide.

With yarn **I** work smaller straight stitches at the tip of each 'toe' for the claws.

Badger

{Meles meles}

The badger, or 'grey' as it was commonly known, because you only see them at night and because that's the only colour you see at night, according to folklore, protects you against all witchcraft. It also used to be said that badgers had legs that were shorter on one side than the other, because they are often seen walking on sloping ground on the sides of hills.

More to colourful 'old grey' than meets the eye, night or day!

FINISHED SIZE

Approx. 20cm (8in) tall, and 39cm (15in) long

YARN

You will need no more than one ball each of:

A: Drops Flora in shade 02 white

B: Drops Brushed Alpaca Silk in shade 01 off white

C: Drops Kid Silk in shade 22 ash grey

D: Drops Kid Silk in shade 02 black

E: Drops Flora in shade 06 black

F: Drops Alpaca in shade 0517 medium grey mix

G: King Cole Luxury Fur in shade 4206 badger

H: Drops Kid Silk in shade 15 dark brown

I: Drops Alpaca in shade 0618 light beige mix

J: James C Brett Faux Fur Chunky in shade H2 grey/white

Unless otherwise stated, multiple strands of yarn are used together throughout this pattern. The exact combinations of yarn to be used are indicated by multiple letters (see How to Use This Book).

NEEDLES

3.75mm and 5mm knitting needles

TENSION

15 rows and 11 stitches over 5cm (2in) with 3.75mm knitting needles

14 rows and 9.5 stitches over 5cm (2in) with 5mm knitting needles

OTHER TOOLS AND MATERIALS

· 1 large safety pin or stitch holder

· 26 locking stitch markers

· 14mm brown toy safety eyes

· Toy filling or yarn/fabric scraps

BEGINNING AT THE MUZZLE

With yarn **AB** and 3.75mm needles, cast on 13 sts.

PM at each end of last row for **Muzzle Marker**.

Row 1 (RS): Kfb, knit to last st, kfb - 15sts

Rows 2-4: Work 3 rows stocking stitch starting with a purl row

Row 5: Kfb, knit to last st, kfb - 17sts

Row 6: P2tog, p to last 2 sts, p2tog -15sts

Row 7: Cast off 5 sts, knit to last 5 sts, cast off last 5 sts and cut yarn - 5sts

BRIDGE OF THE NOSE

With WS facing you, with yarn **AB** and 3.75mm needles, return to the 5 sts.

Row 1 (WS): Pfb, purl to last st, pfb - 7sts

Row 2: K1, kfb, knit to last 2 sts, kfb, k1 -9sts

Rows 3-5: Work 3 rows stocking stitch starting with a purl row

Row 6: K1, kfb, knit to last 2 sts, kfb, k1 - 11sts

Row 7: Pfb, purl to last st, pfb - 13sts

Row 8: K1, kfb, knit to last 2 sts, kfb, k1 - 15sts

PM at each end of last row for **Nose Marker**.

Row 9: Purl

Rows 10-11: Repeat last 2 rows once - 17sts

Rows 12-13: Work 2 rows stocking stitch

Row 14: K2tog, k3, kfb, k5, kfb, knit to last 2 sts, k2tog

Row 15: Purl

Row 16: K2tog, knit to last 2 sts, k2tog - 15sts

Rows 17-23: Work 7 rows stocking stitch starting with a purl row

Row 24: K2tog, knit to last 2 sts, k2tog - 13sts

Row 25: Purl

Rows 26-27: Repeat last 2 rows once - 11sts

Cast off all stitches for Forehead.

PM at each end of last row for **Forehead Marker**.

STRIPES

Badger's Left Stripe

With RS facing you, return to badger's left muzzle, nose and forehead (on your right).

With yarn **CDE** and 3.75mm needles, pick up and knit 12 sts from badger's left **Muzzle Marker** to left **Nose Marker** then pick up and knit 11 sts from badger's left **Nose Marker** to left **Forehead Marker** (see General Techniques) - 23sts.

Work short rows (see General Techniques) to create the left stripe:

Short row 1: P11, W+T

Short row 2: K11

Short row 3: P10, W+T

Short row 4: K10

Short row 5: P9, W+T

Short row 6: K9

Row 1: Purl

Row 2: Cast off 2 sts, knit to end - 21sts.

Row 3: P7, PM for left **Eye Marker**, p4, turn, so knit-side is facing you, cast off 11 sts - 10sts

Badger's Left Cheek

With WS facing you rejoin yarn **CDE** to remaining 10 sts.

Work short rows for left cheek:

Short row 1: P8, W+T

Short row 2: K8

Short row 3: P6, W+T

Short row 4: K6

Short row 5: Purl

Cut **CDE** and join yarn **AB**.

Row 1: K10, pick up and knit 7 sts from left **Eye Marker** to forehead edge - 17sts

Note: The short row ends will line up with the first few cast off stitches to form the eye socket.

Row 2: P17 then pick up and purl 3 sts to left **Muzzle Marker** - 20sts

Rows 3-4: Work 2 rows stocking stitch

Row 5: Cast off 3 sts for chin, knit to end - 17sts

Rows 6-7: Work 2 rows stocking stitch starting with a purl row

Work short rows for left head side:

Short row 1: Pfb, p14, W+T - 18sts

Short row 2: K14, kfb, k1 - 19sts

Short row 3: Pfb, p15, W+T - 20sts

Short row 4: K15, kfb, k1 - 21sts

Cast off all 21 jaw sts purlwise.

PM at start of last row for **Neck Marker**.

Badger's Right Stripe

With RS facing you, return to badger's right forehead, nose and muzzle (on your left).

With yarn **CDE** and 3.75mm needles, pick up and purl 11 sts from badger's right **Forehead Marker** to right **Nose Marker**, then pick up and purl 12 sts from badger's right **Nose Marker** to right **Muzzle Marker** - 23sts

Work short rows to create the right stripe:

Short row 1: K11, W+T

Short row 2: P11

Short row 3: K10, W+T

Short row 4: P10

Short row 5: K9, W+T

Short row 6: P9

Row 1: Knit

Row 2: Cast off 2 sts purlwise, purl to end - 21sts

Row 3: K7, PM for right **Eye Marker**, k4, turn, so purl side is facing you, cast off 11 sts purlwise - 10sts

Badger's Right Cheek

With RS facing you rejoin yarn **CDE** to remaining 10 sts.

Work short rows for right cheek:

Short row 1: K8, W+T

Short row 2: P8

Short row 3: K6, W+T

Short row 4: P6

Short row 5: Knit

Cut **CDE** and join yarn **AB**:

Row 1: P10, pick up and purl 7 sts from right **Eye Marker** to forehead edge - 17sts

Row 2: K17 then pick up and knit 3 sts to right **Muzzle Marker** - 20sts

Rows 3-4: Work 2 rows stocking stitch starting with a purl row

Row 5: Cast off 3 sts purlwise for chin, purl to end - 17sts

Rows 6-7: Work 2 rows stocking stitch

Work short rows for left head side as follows:

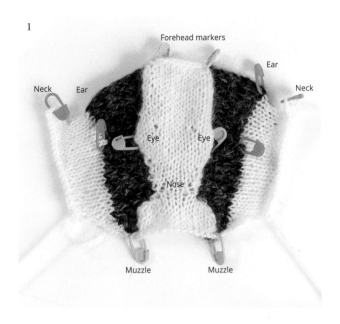

1

Short row 1: Kfb, k14, W+T - 18sts

Short row 2: P14, pfb, k1 - 19sts

Short row 3: Kfb, k15, W+T - 20sts

Short row 4: P15, pfb, k1 - 21sts

Cast off all 21 jaw sts.

PM at start of last row for **Neck Marker**.

Remove **Nose Markers**.

Add Colour to Badger's Right Eyebrow

With RS facing you, return to badger's right eye (on your left).

With yarn **HI** and 3.75mm needles, pick up and knit 6 sts across right eye cast-off edge, ending at right **Eye Marker**.

Cast off purlwise.

Add Colour to Badger's Left Eyebrow

With RS facing you, return to badger's left eye (on your right).

With yarn **HI** and 3.75mm needles, pick up and knit 6 sts across left eye cast-off edge, starting at left **Eye Marker**.

Cast off purlwise.

Remove **Eye Markers**.

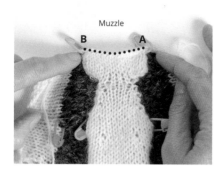

Muzzle

B   A

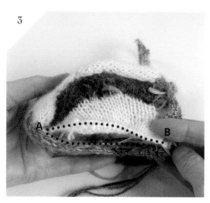

3

A   B

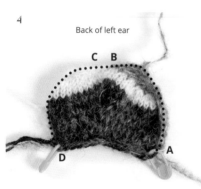

4

Back of left ear

C   B

D   A

5

NECK

With RS facing you, return to the badger's left **Neck Marker** (on your right).

With yarn **BF** and 3.75mm needles, pick up and knit 12 sts along row ends from left **Neck Marker** to left **Forehead Marker**, then pick up and knit 7 sts between left and right **forehead Markers** (across the cast-off edge), then pick up and knit 12 sts along row ends from right **Forehead Marker** to right **Neck Marker** - 31sts

Remove **Forehead Markers**.

Row 1 (WS): Purl

Row 2: Kfb, k9, skpo, PM for badger's left **Ear Back Marker**, k7, PM for badger's right **Ear Back Marker**, k2tog, knit to last st, kfb

Row 3: Purl

Row 4: Kfb, k9, skpo, k7, k2tog, knit to last st, kfb

Rows 5-6: Repeat last 2 rows once

Row 7: P14, p3tog, purl to end - 29sts
Cut **BF** and join yarn **G**.

Rows 8-13: Work 6 rows stocking stitch

Row 14: Switch to 5mm needles and cast on 4 sts, knit to end - 33sts

Row 15: Cast on 4 sts, purl to end - 37sts.
PM at each end of last row for **Front Marker**.

Rows 16-19: Work 4 rows stocking stitch

FORELEGS

Row 20: Cast on 5 sts, k12, [k2tog] twice, k15, [k2tog] twice, knit to end - 38sts
PM at start of last row for left **Foreleg Front Marker**.

Row 21: Cast on 5 sts, purl to end - 43sts
PM at start of last row for right **Foreleg Front Marker**.

Rows 22-29: Work 8 rows stocking stitch
PM at each end of last row for **Foreleg Back Marker**.

BACK AND HIND LEGS

Rows 30-31: Cast off 6 sts at beginning of next two rows - 31sts

Row 32: Kfb, k12, skpo, k1, k2tog, knit to last st, kfb

Row 33: Purl

Row 34: K14, kfb, k1, kfb, knit to end - 33sts

Row 35: Purl

Row 36: K14, kfb, k3, kfb, knit to end - 35sts

Row 37: Purl

Row 38: K14, kfb, k5, kfb, knit to end - 37sts

Row 39: Purl

Row 40: Cast on 2 sts, knit to end - 39sts

Row 41: Cast on 2 sts, purl to end - 41sts

Row 42: Kfb, k1, kfb, knit to last 3 sts, kfb, k1, kfb - 45sts
PM at each end of last row for **Hind Leg Front Marker**.

Rows 43: Purl

Row 44: Kfb, k3, kfb, knit to last 5 sts, kfb, k3, kfb - 49sts

Rows 45: Purl

Row 46: K20, skpo, k5, k2tog, knit to end - 47sts

Rows 47: Purl

Row 48: K20, skpo, k3, k2tog, knit to end - 45sts

Rows 49-51: Work 3 rows stocking stitch starting with a purl row

Separate for Hind Legs

Row 52: K11, PM for left **Tail Marker**, cast off 23 sts, PM for right **Tail Marker**, knit to end - 22sts

Badger's Right Hind Leg

Rows 1-7: Work 7 rows stocking stitch starting with a purl row
Cast off all 11 right hind leg sts.

Badger's Left Hind Leg

With WS facing you, rejoin yarn **G** to 11 sts for left hind leg.

Rows 1-7: Work 7 rows stocking stitch starting with a purl row
Cast off all 11 right hind leg sts.

CHIN AND THROAT

Return to the cast-on edge at the muzzle from the beginning of the pattern.

With RS facing you, with yarn **BC** and 3.75mm needles, pick up and knit 12 sts across the cast-on edge from badger's right **Muzzle Marker** to left **Muzzle Marker** *(see fig. 2, A to B)*.

Remove **Muzzle Markers**.

Chin

Work short rows to create badger's chin:

Short row 1: P7, W+T
Short row 2: K2, W+T
Short row 3: P3, W+T
Short row 4: K4, W+T
Short row 5: P5, W+T
Short row 6: K6, W+T
Short row 7: P7, W+T
Short row 8: K8, W+T
Short row 9: P9, W+T
Short row 10: K10, W+T
Short row 11: Purl to end

Rows 1-10: Work 10 rows stocking stitch

Cut **B** and join **EF** to work with yarn **CEF**.

Rows 11-14: Work 4 rows stocking stitch

Row 15: Kfb, knit to last st, kfb - 14sts

Row 16: Purl

Rows 17-20: Repeat last 2 rows twice - 18sts

PM at each end of last row for **Throat Markers**.

Throat

Cut **F** and join **D** to work with yarn **CDE**.

Row 21: K6, kfb, k4, kfb, knit to end - 20sts

Row 22: Purl

Row 23: K7, kfb, k4, kfb, knit to end - 22sts

Row 24: Purl

Stop knitting here and slip the 22 neck sts onto a stitch holder whilst you sew the jaw seams and knit the ears and eyes.

Join Neck to Throat

Working on one side at a time, with WS together, match the **Throat Marker** with the **Neck Marker** mattress stitch the seam that runs from the muzzle across the cast-off edge from the chin, along the cast-off edge from the jaw to the **Neck and Throat Markers** *(see fig.3, A to B)*.

EARS (MAKE TWO ALIKE)

Outer Ear

With yarn **AB** and 3.75mm needles, cast on 26 sts for edge of outer ear.

Row 1(RS): Knit

Row 2: P12, p2tog, purl to end - 25sts

Cut **AB** join **CDE** to work with yarn **CDE**.

Row 3: K11, k3tog, knit to end - 23sts

Row 4: Purl

Row 5: K10, k3tog, knit to end - 21sts

Row 6: Purl

Row 7: K9, k3tog, knit to end - 19sts

Row 8: Purl

Row 9: K8, k3tog, knit to end - 17sts

Row 10: Purl

Row 11: K7, k3tog, knit to end - 15sts

Cast off purlwise for the ear base.

PM at each end of cast-off for **Ear Base Markers**.

Badger's Left Inner Ear - side one

With RS facing you, with yarn **BB** and 3.75mm needles, pick up and knit 10 sts from the **Ear Base Marker** on your right up to the peak of the ear *(see fig.4, A to B)*.

Rows 1-3: Work 3 rows stocking stitch starting with a purl row.

Cast off.

Badger's Left Inner Ear - side two

With RS facing you, with yarn **BC** and 3.75mm needles, pick up and knit 12 sts from the peak of the ear to the **Ear Base Marker** on your left *(see fig.4, C to D)*.

Rows 1-3: Work 3 rows stocking stitch starting with a purl row.

Cast off.

Badger's Right Inner Ear - side one

With RS facing you, with yarn **BC** and 3.75mm needles, pick up and knit 12 sts from the **Ear Base Marker** on your right up to the peak of the ear.

Rows 1-3: Work 3 rows stocking stitch starting with a purl row.

Cast off.

Badger's Right Inner Ear - side two

With RS facing you, with yarn **BB** and 3.75mm needles, pick up and knit 10 sts from the peak of the ear to the **Ear Base Marker** on your left.

Rows 1-3: Work 3 rows stocking stitch starting with a purl row.

Cast off.

Remove **Ear Base Markers**.

With WS together, flatten the inner ear down to lay inside the outer ear and carefully whip stitch around the cast-off edges and along the row ends of the inner ear so joining to the outer ear.

Attach Ears to the Head

You may find it easier to stuff the head a little first before joining the eyes and the ears.

Working on one ear at a time place the base of the ear onto the head so that the front corners of the ear 'triangle' to fit either side of the top of the badger's black stripe (left ear to left stripe, and right ear to right stripe), and the centre of the ear base matches with the **Ear Back Marker**, then whip stitch neatly and securely to join ear to head *(see fig.5)*.

Remove **Ear Back Markers**.

EYES (MAKE TWO ALIKE)

With yarn **E** and 3.75mm needles, cast on 7 sts.

Rows 1-6: Work 6 rows stocking stitch Cast off.

Sewing the Eyes

With RS together, fold each eye in half at the row ends, cast-on edge to cast-off edge.

Working on one side at a time whip stitch along the row ends. Turn out to RS and open out into an almond-like shape with the seamed ends tucked underneath.

Attach the toy eye in the centre of the knitted eye then insert the knitted eye into the left eye socket beneath the eyebrow *(see fig. 6)*. Using yarn **C** carefully whip stitch around the eye to join it into the eye socket.

NOSE

With yarn **CEH** and 3.75mm needles, cast on 10 sts.

Rows 1-2: Work 2 rows stocking stitch
Row 3: [K2tog, k2] twice, k2tog - 7sts
Row 4: Purl
PM at each end for **Nose Fold Markers**.
Row 5: Cast on 4 sts, knit to end - 11sts
Row 6: Cast on 4 sts, purl to end - 15sts
Rows 7-8: Work 2 rows stocking stitch Cast off.

Sewing on the Nose

Working on one side at a time, with RS together, fold nose at the **Nose Fold Markers**, matching row end of initial cast-on with row end of cast-off. Back stitch to join row ends between initial cast-on and **Nose Fold Marker**, to cast-on edge (from Rows 7 or 8) and row ends before cast-off. Turn out to RS, and stuff the nose a little with yarn **H**.

Remove **Nose Fold Markers**.

Fit the nose over the muzzle and whip stitch in place. The cast-on edge from beginning of nose becomes the top of the nose (at the grey/white colour change), the cast-off edge lies at the mouth seam.

FRONT

With yarn **CDE** 3.75mm needle, slip the 22 neck sts from the stitch holder onto LH needle with RS facing you.

Rows 25-36: Work 12 rows stocking stitch

PM at each end of last row for **Breast Markers**.

Row 37: K2tog, knit to last 2 sts, k2tog - 20sts
Row 38: Purl
Rows 39-44: Repeat last 2 rows three times - 14sts

PM at each end of last row for **Inner Front Foreleg Markers**.

Rows 45-60: Work 16 rows stocking stitch

PM at each end of last row for **Inner Back Foreleg Markers**.

BELLY

Rows 61-72: Work 12 rows stocking stitch

PM at each end of last row for **Inner Hind Leg Markers**.

Rows 73-82: Work 10 rows stocking stitch

Row 83: K2tog, knit to last 2 sts, k2tog - 12sts
Row 84: Purl
Rows 85-92: Repeat last 2 rows four times - 4sts

PM at each end of last row for **Rear End Markers**.

Cast off.

FORELEGS

BADGER'S RIGHT FORELEG

With RS facing you, with yarn **CEHI** and 5mm needles, pick up and knit 8 sts from badger's right **Back Foreleg Marker** to badger's right **Front Foreleg Marker**.

Row 1 (WS): Purl
Row 2: Cast on 10 sts for back of right foreleg, knit to end - 18sts
Row 4: Purl
Row 4: Kfb, knit to last st, kfb - 20sts
Rows 5-9: Work 5 rows stocking stitch starting with a purl row
Row 10: Kfb, knit to last st, kfb - 22sts
Cut **E** and join **B** to work with yarn **BCHI**.

Work short rows for badger's front paw - side one:

Short row 1: P1, W+T
Short row 2: K1
Short row 3: P2, W+T
Short row 4: K2
Short row 5: P3, W+T
Short row 6: K3
Short row 7: P4, W+T
Short row 8: K4
Short row 9: P5, W+T
Short row 10: K5
Short row 11: P6, W+T
Short row12: K6
Short row 13: P7, W+T
Short row 14: K7
Cast off 14sts purlwise, purl to end - 8sts
Work short rows for badger's front paw - side two:

Short row 1: K1, W+T
Short row 2: P1
Short row 3: K2, W+T
Short row 4: P2
Short row 5: K3, W+T
Short row 6: P3
Short row 7: K4, W+T
Short row 8: P4
Short row 9: K5, W+T
Short row 10: P5
Short row 11: K6, W+T
Short row12: P6
Short row 13: K7, W+T
Short row 14: P7
Cast off all 8 sts.

BADGER'S LEFT FORELEG

With WS facing you, with yarn **CEHI** and 5mm needles, pick up and purl 8 sts from left **Back Foreleg Marker** to left **Front Foreleg Marker**.

Row 1 (RS): Knit
Row 2: Cast on 10 sts for back of right foreleg, purl to end - 18sts
Row 4: Knit
Row 4: Pfb, purl to last st, pfb - 20sts
Rows 5-9: Work 5 rows stocking stitch
Row 10: Pfb, purl to last st, pfb - 22sts
Cut **E** and join **B** to work with yarn **BCHI**.

Work short rows for badger's front paw - side one:

Short row 1: K1, W+T
Short row 2: P1
Short row 3: K2, W+T
Short row 4: P2
Short row 5: K3, W+T
Short row 6: P3
Short row 7: K4, W+T
Short row 8: P4
Short row 9: K5, W+T
Short row 10: P5
Short row 11: K6, W+T
Short row12: P6
Short row 13: K7, W+T
Short row 14: P7
Cast off 14sts, knit to end - 8sts
Work short rows for badger's front paw - side two:

Short row 1: P1, W+T
Short row 2: K1
Short row 3: P2, W+T
Short row 4: K2
Short row 5: P3, W+T
Short row 6: K3
Short row 7: P4, W+T
Short row 8: K4
Short row 9: P5, W+T
Short row 10: K5
Short row 11: P6, W+T
Short row12: K6
Short row 13: P7, W+T
Short row 14: K7
Cast off all 8 sts purlwise.

Join Foreleg Seam

Working on one foreleg at a time, with WS together fold the leg in half matching the shape created by short rows.

Mattress stitch to join across cast-off edge, then along short row ends, and finally join row ends from the back of the leg (this seam lies at the front of the leg).

Leave the cast-on edge from foreleg back. You'll join this to the belly later.

Flatten the paler part of the foot, and stuff the leg.

With yarn **B** work four straight stitches for the paw claws over the paler part of the foot.

INNER HIND LEGS

Badger's Left Inner Hind Leg

With RS of belly part facing you, with yarn **CEHI** and 5mm needles, pick up and knit 11 sts from Badger's left **Rear End Marker** to left **Inner Hind Leg Marker**.

Row 1 (WS): Purl
Row 2: Kfb, knit to end - 12sts
Rows 3-6: Repeat last 2 rows twice - 14sts
Row 7: Purl
Row 8: Kfb, knit to last 2 sts, k2tog
Rows 9-12: Repeat last 2 rows twice
Row 13: Purl
PM at end of last row for **Foot Marker**.
Cast off all sts.

Badger's Right Inner Hind Leg

With RS of belly part facing you, with yarn **CEHI** and 5mm needles, pick up and knit 11 sts from Badger's right **Inner Hind Leg Marker** to right **Rear End Marker**.

Row 1 (WS): Purl
Row 2: Knit to last st, kfb - 12sts
Rows 3-6: Repeat last 2 rows twice - 14sts
Row 7: Purl
Row 8: K2tog, knit to last st, kfb
Rows 9-12: Repeat last 2 rows twice
Row 13: Purl
PM at start of last row for **Foot Marker**.
Cast off all sts.

7

Neck to throat marker

Breast to front marker

Inner foreleg front to foreleg front marker

Inner hind leg front to hind leg front marker

Inner foreleg back to foreleg back marker

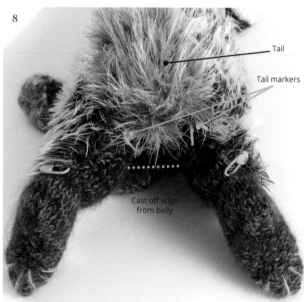

8

Tail

Tail markers

Cast off edge from belly

BODY SEAMS

Join Back to Belly and Hind Legs

Working on one side at a time, match the **Neck Marker** to the **Throat Marker** and the **Front Marker** to the **Breast Marker**, and mattress stitch to join seam that runs from the **Neck Marker** to the **Front Marker** (*see fig.7*).

Remove **Neck**, **Throat** and **Breast Markers**.

Match the **Foreleg Front Marker** to the **Inner Foreleg Front Marker**, and mattress stitch to join seam that runs from the **Front Marker** to the **Foreleg Front Marker**.

Match the **Foreleg Back Marker** with the **Inner Foreleg Back Marker** and mattress stitch to join the belly with the cast-on edge from the back of the foreleg.

Remove **Front**, **Foreleg Front**, **Inner Foreleg Front**, and **Inner Foreleg Back Markers**.

Match the **Hind Leg Front Marker** with the **Inner Hind Leg Marker** and mattress stitch the seam that runs from the **Foreleg Back Marker** to the **Hind Leg Front Marker**.

Remove **Foreleg Back** and **Inner Hind Leg Markers**.

Join Hind Legs to Inner Hind Legs

Working on one hind leg at a time, with WS together, match the cast-off edges from the inner and outer hind leg, and mattress stitch to join for paw seam.

Now ease together and mattress stitch to join from **Hind Leg Front Marker** to paw seam.

Match the **Tail Marker** with the **Rear End Marker** and mattress stitch to join from **Tail Marker** to paw seam.

Leave the cast-off edge between the **Tail Markers** open. This is where you'll pick up sts for the tail.

Tuck in yarn ends and stuff the head and body before completing the hind leg seam on the second side.

Remove **Hind Leg Front** and **Rear End Markers**.

BADGER'S HIND LEG FEET (MAKE TWO ALIKE)

With yarn **CEHI** and 5mm needles cast on 20 sts.
Rows 1-2: Work 2 rows stocking stitch
Row 3: Kfb, knit to last st, kfb - 22sts
Row 4: Purl
Rows 5-12: Repeat last 2 rows four times - 30sts
Work short rows to shape paw - side one
Short row 1: K9, W+T
Short row 2: P9
Short row 3: K8, W+T
Short row 4: P8
Short row 5: K7, W+T
Short row 6: P7
Short row 7: K6, W+T
Short row 8: P6
Short row 9: K5, W+T
Short row 10: P5
Cast off 20 sts, knit to end - 10sts.

Work short rows to shape paw - side two

Short row 1: P9, W+T
Short row 2: K9
Short row 3: P8, W+T
Short row 4: K8
Short row 5: P7, W+T
Short row 6: K7
Short row 7: P6, W+T
Short row 8: K6
Short row 9: P5, W+T
Short row 10: K5

Cast off all sts purlwise.

With WS together, fold foot in half across the cast-on edge. Mattress stitch to join the seam across the rows ends at the front of the foot then across the cast-off edges at the base of the foot. Flatten the front of the foot, and then stuff the ankle part.

Place the open edge, the cast-on edge, over the paw seam on the hind leg with the back of the foot aligned with the **Foot Marker**.

With yarn **B** work five straight stitches for the paw claws.

Remove **Foot Markers**.

TAIL

With RS facing you, with yarn **J** and 5mm needles, pick up and knit 19 sts between the two **Tail Markers**.

Rows 1-15: Work 15 rows stocking stitch starting with a purl row
Row 16: K2tog, knit to last 2 sts, k2tog - 17sts
Row 17: Purl
Rows 18-21: Repeat last 2 rows twice - 13sts
PM at each end of last row for **Tail Fold Markers**.
Rows 22-23: Work 2 rows stocking stitch
Row 24: Kfb, knit to last st, kfb - 15sts
Row 25: Purl
Rows 26-27: Repeat last 2 rows once - 17sts
Rows 28-29: Work 2 rows stocking stitch
Row 30: K2tog, knit to last 2 sts, k2tog - 15sts
Rows 31-33: Work 3 rows stocking stitch starting with a purl row
Row 34: K2tog, knit to last 2 sts, k2tog - 13sts
Rows 35-37: Work 3 rows stocking stitch starting with a purl row
Row 38: K2tog, knit to last 2 sts, k2tog - 11sts
Row 39: Purl
Row 40: K2tog, knit to last 2 sts, k2tog - 9sts
Row 41: Purl
Row 42: K2tog, knit to last 2 sts, k2tog - 7sts
Cast off.

Complete any stuffing into the body.

Fold tail at the **Tail Fold Markers**.

Ease together then whip stitch the tail cast-off edge to the belly cast-off edge *(see fig.8)*.

Whip stitch to join along the tail sides. The tail is not stuffed.

Remove **Tail Fold** and **Tail Markers**.

General Techniques

Short Rows - Wrap and Turn

On a knit row:

Step 1: Bring working yarn to the front of the work, slip next stitch purlwise onto the RH needle *(see fig. 1)*.

Step 2: Take working yarn to the back of the work *(see fig. 2)*.

Step 3: Slip the wrapped stitch back onto the LH needle *(see fig. 3)*.

Step 4: Turn the knitting to work back in the other direction.

On a purl row:

Step 1: Take working yarn to the back of the work, slip next stitch purlwise onto the RH needle *(see fig. 4)*.

Step 2: Bring working yarn to the front of the work *(see fig. 5)*.

Step 3: Slip the wrapped stitch back onto the LH needle *(see fig. 6)*.

Step 4: Turn the knitting to work back in the other direction.

There is no need to pick up the wraps on subsequent rows for these patterns.

1

2
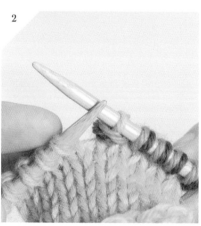

3

4

5

6

7

10

Pick Up and Knit or Purl

Pick up and knit on the RS:

Step 1: Insert RH needle into a space at the edge of the knitting from front to back *(see fig. 7)*.

Step 2: Loop yarn around the needle *(see fig. 8)*.

Step 3: Pull the yarn through, just as though you are knitting *(see fig. 9)*.

Repeat steps 1 and 2 until the required number of stitches have been picked up.

Pick up and purl on the WS:

Step 1: Insert RH needle into a space at the edge of the knitting from back to front *(see fig. 10)*.

Step 2: Loop yarn around the needle *(see fig. 11)*.

Step 3: Pull the yarn through, just as though you are purling *(see fig. 12)*.

Repeat steps 1 and 2 until the required number of stitches have been picked up.

8

11

9

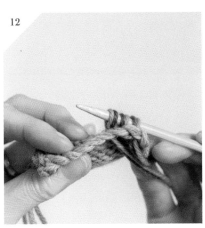

12

i-cord

i-cord is usually worked on between 2 and 5 stitches.

Step 1: With RS facing you, slip the specified number of stitches from RH needle to LH needle, then knit these stitches.

Repeat step 1 until the i-cord is the required length.

After a few rows, you will see that the strand across the back pulls the edges together to form a tube *(see fig. 13)*.

13

About the author

If there's one constant throughout Claire Garland's life, it's her need to create.

Claire lives with her family, in a little white cottage tucked away in a corner of Cornwall, surrounded by woods and fields. Here she knits at her kitchen table, inspired by the fauna which surrounds her home.

Claire started knitting toys many years ago, with characterful bears and dolls for her three children.

More recently she decided to create as realistic a rabbit as possible given the constraints of yarn and knitting. At around this time Claire also set up an Instagram account and tried her first bunny out on her small following – an instant hit – so another bunny followed then another and another until she had a positive 'fluffle' of bunnies and a substantial following of knitted bunny enthusiasts.

This has now developed into a veritable menagerie: foxes, mice, birds, deer, and there are still many more creatures in the future.

You can follow Claire and her creations on Instagram at @dotpebbles_knits.

Thank you

I would like to thank the following people without whom this book would not be as beautiful as it is:

Sarah Callard and all the team at David and Charles for very kindly inviting me to write it in the first place. I'm truly grateful.

The design team at D&C for pulling the whole book together so beautifully and being patient with me (all those step photos). I'd particularly like to thank Sam for the styling here in Cornwall, especially around that perfect duck pond!

Jason Jenkins, wildlife photographer extraordinaire. I'm in awe of the way you've brought these creatures to life with your lighting and your awesome photographic skills.

Pru for art-directing, with such stunning and creative styling and props.

Charlie, tech editor – what can I say? I have never met anyone so organised and methodical and so incredibly tolerant all at the same time. You've changed the way I work!

Wool Warehouse for supplying all that gorgeous, gorgeous yarn. Worth writing a book for!

To the brilliant knitting ladies Eileen and Wendy (my mum). I am so grateful to you both for helping me out with the step knitting – it couldn't have been done in time otherwise!

Of course, my lovely family get mention – for just being who they are and always believing in me.

And my final word of praise belongs to all my friends on Instagram and Facebook, thank you all for jollying along with me – this book is for you!

Suppliers

Yarn

All the yarns used in this book can be bought from woolwarehouse.co.uk, who ship internationally.

For other suppliers, please check the yarn manufacturers websites:

Drops - garnstudio.com

Rico Design - rico-design.com

James C Brett - jamescbrett.co.uk

King Cole - kingcole.com

Toy eyes

Cello Express - ebaystores.co.uk/Celloexpress

Glasseyes.com - glasseyes.com

Mister Eyes - etsy.com/shop/MisterEyes

Shamrock Rose - etsy.com/shop/ShamrockRose

Toy filling

Habbyboy - ebaystores.co.uk/Habbyboy

Christie Bears Ltd - christiebears.com

Wire legs, florist's tape and wire

The Makerss - themakerss.co.uk and etsy.com/shop/TheMakerss

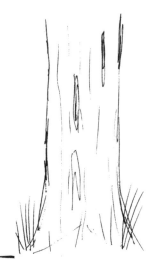

A DAVID AND CHARLES BOOK
© David and Charles, Ltd 2020

David and Charles is an imprint of David and Charles, Ltd
Suite A, Tourism House, Pynes Hill, Exeter, EX2 5WS

First published in the UK and USA in 2020

A catalogue record for this book is available from the British Library.

ISBN-13: 9781446308103 paperback
ISBN-13: 9781446379691 EPUB
ISBN-13: 9781446379684 PDF

This book has been printed on paper from approved suppliers and made from pulp from sustainable sources.

Printed in Bosnia and Herzegovina by GPS for:
David and Charles, Ltd
Suite A, Tourism House, Pynes Hill, Exeter, EX2 5WS

10 9 8 7 6 5 4

Publishing Director: Ame Verso
Senior Commissioning Editor: Sarah Callard
Managing Editor: Jeni Hennah
Project Editor: Charlotte Monckton
Design Manager: Anna Wade
Designer: Sam Staddon
Art Direction: Prudence Rogers
Photographer: Jason Jenkins
Production Manager: Beverley Richardson

David and Charles publishes high-quality books on a wide range of subjects. For more information visit www.davidandcharles.com.

Share your makes with us on social media using #dandcbooks and follow us on Facebook and Instagram by searching for @dandcbooks.

Layout of the digital edition of this book may vary depending on reader hardware and display settings.

Index